501

Grammar and Writing Questions

4th Edition

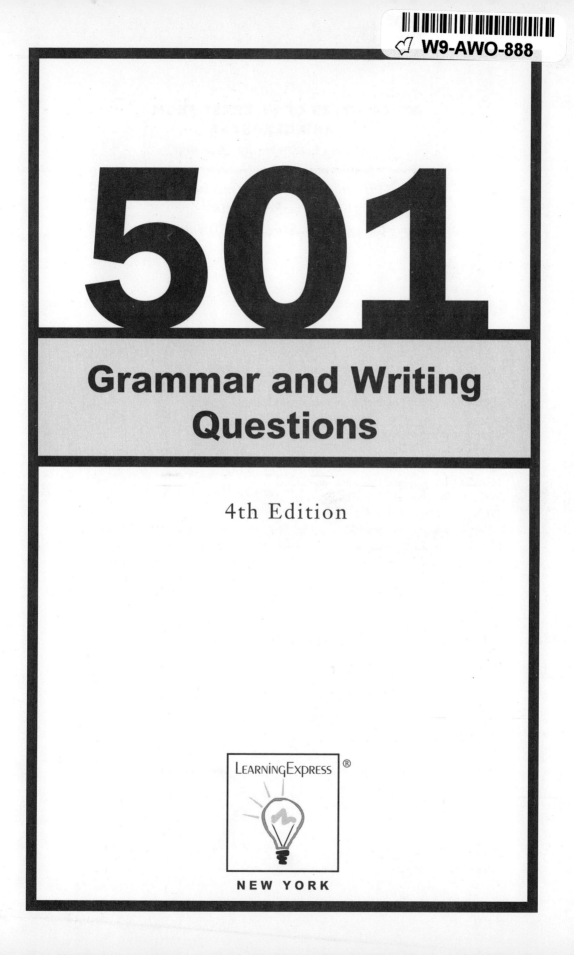

LearningExpress ®

NEW YORK

OTHER TITLES OF INTEREST FROM LEARNINGEXPRESS

501 Reading Comprehension Questions
501 Critical Reading Questions
501 Sentence Completion Questions
501 Word Analogy Questions
Reading Comprehension Success in 20 Minutes a Day

Published in the United States by LearningExpress, LLC, New York.

Library of Congress Cataloging-in-Publication Data:

501 grammar and writing questions. — 4th ed.
  p. cm.
 Spine title: 501 grammar & writing questions
 Includes bibliographical references and index.
 ISBN-13: 978-1-57685-748-9 (alk. paper)
 ISBN-10: 1-57685-748-4 (alk. paper)
1. English language—Grammar—Examinations, questions, etc. 2. English language—Rhetoric—Examinations, questions, etc. 3. Report writing—Examinations, questions, etc. I. LearningExpress (Organization) II. Title: Five hundred one grammar and writing questions. III. Title: Five hundred and one grammar and writing questions. IV. Title: 501 grammar & writing questions.
 PE1112.A15 2010
 428.2'076--dc22

                        2010010694

Printed in the United States of America

9 8 7 6 5 4 3 2 1

Fourth Edition

For more information or to place an order, contact LearningExpress at:
  2 Rector Street
  26th Floor
  New York, NY 10006

Or visit us at:
  www.learnatest.com

Contents

Introduction

This book can be used alone, along with another writing-skills text of your choice, or in combination with the LearningExpress publication, *Writing Skills Success in 20 Minutes a Day*. It will give you practice dealing with capitalization, punctuation, basic grammar, sentence structure, organization, paragraph development, and essay writing. It is designed to be used by individuals working on their own and for teachers or tutors helping students learn or review basic writing skills. Additionally, practicing with *501 Grammar and Writing Questions* will greatly alleviate writing anxiety.

Many people grimace when faced with grammar exercises. But in order to communicate with others, pass tests, and get your point across in writing, using words and punctuation effectively is a necessary skill. Maybe you're one of the millions of people who found memorizing grammar rules tedious as a student in elementary or high school. Maybe you were confused by all of the *exceptions* to those rules. Maybe you thought they would just come naturally as you continued to write and speak.

First, know you are not alone. It is true that some people work very hard to understand the rules, while others seem to have a natural gift for writing. And that's okay; we all have unique talents. Still, it's a fact that most jobs today require good communication skills, including writing. The good news is that grammar and writing skills can be developed with practice.

Learn by doing. It's an old lesson, tried and true. The 501 grammar and writing questions included in these pages are designed to provide you with lots of practice. As you work through each set of questions, you'll be gaining a solid understanding of basic grammar and usage rules. And all without memorizing! This book will help you improve your language skills through encouragement, not frustration.

An Overview

501 Grammar and Writing Questions is divided into six sections:

Section 1: Mechanics: Capitalization and Punctuation
Section 2: Sentence Structure
Section 3: Agreement
Section 4: Modifiers
Section 5: Paragraph Development
Section 6: Essay Questions

Each section is subdivided into short sets consisting of 8–20 questions.

The book is specifically organized to help you build confidence as you further develop your written-language skills. *501 Grammar and Writing Questions* begins with the basic mechanics of capitalization and punctuation, and then moves on to grammar and sentence structure. By the time you reach the section on paragraph development, you will have practiced on almost 300 questions. You will then continue practicing the skills that you've already begun to master in the previous four sections, this time in combination. When you get to the last section, you'll be ready to write your own essays.

How to Use This Book

Whether you're working alone or helping someone brush up on grammar and usage, this book will give you the opportunity to practice, practice, practice.

Working on Your Own

If you are working alone to review the basics or prepare for a test in connection with a job or school, you will probably want to use this book in combination with a basic grammar and usage text, or with *Writing Skills Success in 20 Minutes a Day*. If you're fairly sure of your basic language-mechanics skills, however, you can use *501 Grammar and Writing Questions* by itself.

Use the answer key at the end of the book to find out if you chose the right answer, and also to learn how to tackle similar kinds of questions next time. Every answer is explained. Make sure you understand the explanations—usually by going back to the questions—before moving on to the next set.

Tutoring Others

This book will work well in combination with almost any basic grammar and usage text. You will probably find it most helpful to give students a brief lesson in the particular skill they'll be learning—capitalization, punctuation, subject-verb agreement, pronoun agreement, sentence structure, style—and then have them spend the remainder of the session answering the questions in the sets. You will want to impress upon them the importance of learning by doing, checking their answers, and reading the explanations carefully. Make sure they understand a particular set of questions before you assign the next one.

Additional Resources

For more detailed explanations of English grammar and usage rules, you may want to buy—or borrow from the library—one or more of the following books:

Action Grammar: Fast, No-Hassle Answers on Everyday Usage and Punctuation by Joanne Feierman (Fireside)

The American Heritage Book of English Usage: A Practical and Authoritative Guide to Contemporary English (Houghton Mifflin)

The Blue Book of Grammar and Punctuation: The Mysteries of Grammar and Punctuation Revealed by Jane Straus (Jane Straus Books)

Grammatically Correct: The Writer's Essential Guide to Punctuation, Spelling, Style, Usage and Grammar by Anne Stilman (Writer's Digest Books)

The Oxford Dictionary of American Usage and Style by Bryan A. Garner (Berkley Publishing Group)

Woe is I: The Grammarphobes Guide to Better English in Plain English, 2nd Edition, by Patricia T. O'Conner (Riverhead Books)

Writing Skills Success in 20 Minutes a Day, 3rd Edition (LearningExpress)

Grammar Success in 20 Minutes a Day, 2nd Edition (LearningExpress)

Grammar Essentials, 3rd Edition (LearningExpress)

Mechanics: Capitalization and Punctuation

Every sentence begins with a capital, so the how-tos of capitalization seem like a logical place to begin learning about language mechanics. When doing the exercises in this section, refer to the following checklist. Matching your answer to a rule will reinforce the mechanics of writing and secure that knowledge for you.

Capitalization Checklist

✓ The first word of every sentence→**Y**es, *we do carry the matching bed skirt.*
✓ The first word of a quoted sentence (not just a quoted phrase)→*And with great flourish, he sang,* "**O** *beautiful for spacious skies, for amber waves of grain!*"
✓ The specific name of a person (and his or her title), a place, or a thing (otherwise known as *proper nouns*). *Proper nouns* include specific locations and geographic regions; political, social, and athletic organizations and agencies; historical events; documents and periodicals; nationalities and their languages; religions, their members and their deities; brand or trade names; and holidays.

✓ The abbreviation for *proper nouns*. Government agencies are probably the most frequently abbreviated. Remember to capitalize each letter.→*The* **CIA** *makes me feel very secure.*

✓ Adjectives (descriptive words) derived from *proper nouns*.
   Ex: **A**merica *(proper noun)*→the **A**merican *(adjective) flag*

✓ The *pronoun* **I**.

✓ The most important words in a title→*Last March, I endured a twenty-hour public reading of* **A T**ale of **T**wo **C**ities.

Punctuation Checklist
Periods

✓ At the end of a declarative sentence (sentence that makes a statement)→*Today, I took a walk to nowhere.*

✓ At the end of a command or request→*Here's a cloth. Now gently burp the baby on your shoulder.*

✓ At the end of an indirect question→*Jane asked if I knew where she had left her keys.*

✓ Before a decimal number→*Statisticians claim that the average family raises 2.5 children.*

✓ Between dollars and cents→*I remember when $1.50 could buy the coolest stuff.*

✓ After an initial in a person's name→*You are Sir James W. Dewault, are you not?*

✓ After an abbreviation→*On Jan. 12, I leave for Africa.*

Question Marks

✓ At the end of a question→*Why do you look so sad?*

✓ Inside a quotation mark when the quotation is a question→*She asked, "Why do you look so sad?"*

Exclamation Points

✓ At the end of a word, phrase, or sentence filled with emotion→*Hurry up! I cannot be late for the meeting!*

✓ Inside a quotation mark when the quotation is an exclamation→*The woman yelled, "Hurry up! I cannot be late for the meeting!"*

Quotation Marks

✓ When directly quoting dialogue, not when paraphrasing→*Hamlet says, "To be, or not to be. That is the question."*

✓ For titles of chapters, articles, short stories, poems, songs, or periodicals→*My favorite poem is "The Road Not Taken."*

Semicolons

✓ Between two independent clauses (an independent clause is a complete thought. It has a subject and a predicate. See Section 2.)→*Edward joined the basketball team; remarkably, the 5´4˝ young man excelled at the sport.*

✓ Between elements in a series that uses commas →*The possible dates for the potluck dinner are Thursday, June 5; Saturday, June 7; or Monday, June 9.*

Colons

✓ Before a list→*Grandma brought Chloe's favorite three sweets: chocolate kisses, Tootsie Rolls, and a Snickers bar.*

✓ Between titles and subtitles→*Finding Your Dream Home: A Buyer's Guide.*

✓ Between volumes and page numbers→*Marvel Comics 21:24*

✓ Between chapters and verse→*Job 4:12*

✓ Between hours and minutes→*It's 2:00 A.M.*—time to sleep.

Apostrophes

✓ Contractions: A contraction is a combination of two words into one, such as *don't* (do not) and *it's* (it is). The apostrophe indicates that some letters have been omitted: *do + not* = don[o]t; *it + is* = it[i]s→*I can't go with you.*

✓ Possessives: A possessive is a word that shows ownership of some sort. *The dog's bowl* tells us that the bowl belongs to the dog, and we make *dog* possessive by adding *'s*. If we have two dogs, however, we already have an *s* to indicate that there is more than one dog (plural). If the two dogs own the bowl, we make it possessive by adding an apostrophe *after* the s: *the dogs' bowl*→*This is Mike's house. These are the students' desks.*

✓ Exception: The one exception to the above rules is *its* and *it's*. The apostrophe in *it's* indicates a contraction of *it is*. To make *it* possessive, therefore, we do not use an apostrophe: *its bowl*→*I think it's* (it is) *going to rain. The dog ate from its* (possessive) *bowl.*

Commas

✓ Between items in dates and addresses→*Michael arrived at Ellis Island, New York, on February 14, 1924.*

✓ Between words in a list→*The university hired a woman to direct the Bursar's, Financial Aid, and Registrar's offices.*

✓ Between equally important adjectives (be careful not to separate adjectives that describe each other)→*The reporter spoke with several intense, talented high school athletes.*

✓ After words that precede a direct quotation→*David whined, "I am famished."*

✓ In a quotation that precedes a tag and is not a question or an exclamation→*"I am famished," whined David.*

✓ Around nonessential clauses, parenthetical phrases, and appositives. (A nonessential or nonrestrictive clause is a word or group of words that is not necessary for the sentence's completion; a parenthetical phrase interrupts the flow of a sentence; and an appositive is a word or group of words that renames the preceding noun)→*Matt's mother, Janie* (appositive), *who has trouble with directions* (nonessential clause), *had to ask for help.*

✓ Before or after a dependent clause. (We will learn about dependent clauses in Section 2.)→*We checked our luggage* (independent clause), *hoping for the best* (dependent clause).

✓ Before conjunctions. (Conjunctions are words that link two independent clauses together)→*Drew wanted to experience ballroom dancing before his wedding, so he signed up for lessons at a local hall.*

VERBS

Words that describe an action. A few examples:

drive fast	*sleep* well
jump high	*play* ball

SET 1 (Answers begin on page 157.)

For the following questions, choose the lettered part of the sentence that contains a word that needs a capital letter. If no additional words should be capitalized, choose choice **e**. Refer to the checklist at the beginning of the chapter if you want to be certain about your answer.

1. my cousin | George won | the blue ribbon | in the contest. | None
      a   b   c   d   e

2. Professor Smith | teaches french literature | at the local
           a   b   c
   | community college. | None
      d   e

3. Michael Blake, jr., | is such an accomplished golfer | that he won
         a   b   c
   three tournaments | in a row. | None
          d   e

4. Catherine complained loudly, | "why can't you ever | pick me up
           a.   b   c
   on time | in the morning?" | None
        d   e

5. The Declaration of Independence | is one of the most important
            a   b
   | documents in the history | of the United States. | None
       c   d   e

6. Sally's Sweet shop, | one of the oldest businesses in town, | is
       a   b
   located on one of the main streets | of Millersville. | None
       c   d   e

7. My first childhood pet, | a gray cat named otis, | was given to me
          a   b   c
   as a gift | on my fifth birthday. | None
         d   e

8. The local elementary school | is organizing a screening | of the
          a   b
   movie toy story |as a fundraiser. | None
       c   d   e

SET 2 (Answers begin on page 157.)
Choose the punctuation mark that is needed in each of the following sentences. If no additional punctuation is needed, choose choice **e**.

9. "It isn't fair!" shouted Martin. Coach Lewis never lets me start the game!"
   a. .
   b. ,
   c. !
   d. "
   e. none

10. Maureen's three sisters, Molly, Shannon, and Patricia are all spending the summer at their grandmother's beach house.
    a. ;
    b. —
    c. !
    d. ,
    e. none

11. For the centerpieces, the florist recommended the following flowers daisies, tulips, daffodils, and hyacinths.
    a. :
    b. ,
    c. .
    d. ;
    e. none

12. "What time is supper" George asked.
    a. ;
    b. ,
    c. ?
    d. :
    e. None

13. Everyone was shocked when Max Smithfield—a studious, extremely bright high school senior decided that college was not for him.
   a. ;
   b. ,
   c. —
   d. :
   e. none

14. Kims assistant, usually so reliable, has been late for work three
times this week, without any excuse.
   a. '
   b. ,
   c. ;
   d. .
   e. none

15. Our class president, Horace Landek, called the meeting to order
at 4:00.
   a. ,
   b. ;
   c. —
   d. .
   e. none

16. "I remember" Luis recollected, "the first time I was allowed to
walk home from school by myself."
   a. ?
   b. ,
   c. :
   d. ;
   e. none

17. Madeline Larkin our office manager, is the most organized person
I've ever known.
   a. :
   b. ;
   c. —
   d. ,
   e. none

18. I spend most of my time at the gym on the treadmill walking is my favorite form of exercise.

   a. ,

   b. ?

   c. ;

   d. !

   e. none

SET 3 (Answers begin on page 158.)

Choose the answer that shows the best punctuation for the underlined part of the sentence. If the sentence is correct as is, choose choice **e**.

19. Simone bought three new pairs of <u>shoes even though she</u> had put herself on a tight budget just last week.

   a. shoes, even though, she

   b. shoes, even though she

   c. shoes. Even though she

   d. shoes; even though she

   e. correct as is

20. Most residents of the building have <u>air conditioners however I've</u> always found that a ceiling fan is sufficient.

   a. air conditioners however: I've

   b. air conditioners, however, I've

   c. air conditioners however, I've

   d. air conditioners; however, I've

   e. correct as is

21. "Are you <u>OK," asked Timothy, "Are</u> you sure you don't want to sit down and rest for a while?"

   a. OK?" asked Timothy. "Are

   b. OK?" asked Timothy, "Are

   c. OK," asked Timothy? "Are

   d. OK?" asked Timothy? "Are

   e. correct as is

22. The owners of the restaurant <u>maintain that only</u> organic ingredients are used in their kitchen.
   a. maintain, that only
   b. maintain that, only
   c. maintain: that only
   d. maintain—that only
   e. correct as is

23. Before the student could be hired by the <u>company, the students</u> adviser had to provide a letter of recommendation.
   a. company the students
   b. company, the student's
   c. company, the students'
   d. company the students'
   e. correct as is

24. The <u>volunteers who would like to work the morning shift</u> should sign their name on this sheet.
   a. volunteers, who would like to work the morning shift
   b. volunteers who would like to work the morning shift,
   c. volunteers, who would like to work the morning shift,
   d. volunteers who, would like to work the morning shift,
   e. correct as is

25. The employees asked whether the company would be offering tuition <u>reimbursement within the next three years?</u>
   a. reimbursement within the next three years!
   b. reimbursement, within the next three years.
   c. reimbursement within the next three years.
   d. reimbursement, within the next three years?
   e. correct as is

26. The <u>sky is blue</u>, but I hear thunder in the distance.
   a. sky, is blue,
   b. sky is blue;
   c. sky is blue
   d. sky is, blue;
   e. correct as is

27. <u>George as captain of the team</u> called the plays.
   a. George, as captain of the team,
   b. George as captain of the team,
   c. George, as captain of the team
   d. George, as captain of the team?
   e. correct as is

28. They met for the first time on <u>August 27, 1972 in Seattle, Washington.</u>
   a. August 27 1972 in Seattle, Washington.
   b. August 27 1972, in Seattle Washington.
   c. August 27, 1972 in Seattle, Washington.
   d. August 27, 1972, in Seattle, Washington.
   e. correct as is

SET 4 (Answers begin on page 158.)
For each question, find the sentence that has a mistake in capitalization or punctuation. If you find no mistakes, mark choice **d**.

29. **a.** My least favorite season is Winter.
   b. Next Friday, Uncle Jake is coming to visit.
   c. Maureen served as treasurer for the women's organization.
   d. No mistakes.

30. **a.** "Can you attend next week's meeting?" she asked.
   b. His new car was damaged in the accident.
   c. The girls' giggled through the whole movie.
   d. No mistakes.

31. **a.** Leo told her, to call the customer service department in the morning.
   b. She put up signs all over town, but she didn't get any response.
   c. Occasionally, her neighbors ask her to feed their cat.
   d. No mistakes.

32. **a.** Did you see the movie *Shrek*?
   b. She was given an award by mayor Chambers.
   c. Math and science are my two best subjects.
   d. No mistakes.

33.   **a.** My cat loves to sit in the window.
     b. The weather has been cold lately.
     c. Deborah moved to south Dakota.
     d. No mistakes.

34.   **a.** I'm wondering when the doctor will call?
     b. Yesterday, Bill turned 40.
     c. Benjamin, my younger brother, joined the Army.
     d. No mistakes.

35.   **a.** The school bus was late because of snow.
     b. Why did you say that, since it isn't true.
     c. Cover your mouth when you sneeze!
     d. No mistakes.

36.   **a.** Rhode Island is the smallest State.
     b. "I know the answer to that!" Phyllis shouted.
     c. When you're done, put your pencils down and look up.
     d. No mistakes.

37.   **a.** Please walk the dog while you're out.
     b. Lets go to the movies!
     c. Cassandra does not like spinach.
     d. No mistakes.

38.   **a.** Bill seeing Betty walked the other way.
     b. This is the dog's bowl.
     c. It's a long way from home.
     d. No mistakes.

39.   **a.** Don't stand in my way.
     b. Cecilia and I fought our way through the crowd.
     c. The vegetables were old rubbery and tasteless.
     d. No mistakes.

40.   **a.** Remember to walk the dog.
     b. "Don't run"! Mr. Ellington shouted.
     c. It's supposed to snow today and tomorrow.
     d. No mistakes.

41. **a.** Charleen's parents worried whenever she drove the car.
     b. Who designed the Brooklyn Bridge?
     c. Diseases like Smallpox and Polio have been eradicated.
     d. No mistakes.

42. **a.** Can you find the Indian ocean on this map?
     b. Which river, the Nile or the Amazon, is longer?
     c. Lerner Avenue runs into the Thompson Parkway.
     d. No mistakes.

43. **a.** He's the best dancer in the school.
     b. We were planning to go, but the meeting was canceled.
     c. "Okay," she said, I'll go with you."
     d. No mistakes.

44. **a.** Does Judge Parker live on your street?
     b. Twenty government officials met to deal with Wednesday's crisis.
     c. The Mayor spoke at a news conference this morning.
     d. No mistakes.

45. **a.** My brother, Isaac, is the best player on the team.
     b. Because of the high cost; we decided not to go.
     c. Where's your new puppy?
     d. No mistakes.

46. **a.** I have learned to appreciate Mozart's music.
     b. My cousin Veronica is studying to be a Veterinarian.
     c. Mr. Shanahan is taller than Professor Martin.
     d. No mistakes.

47. **a.** "You look just like your mother," Ms. Jones told me.
     b. "Please be careful," he said.
     c. Tyler asked, "why do I have to go to bed so early?"
     d. No mistakes.

48.   **a.** Do you prefer root beer or orange soda?
     b. In which year did world war II end?
     c. I like to study the geography of the Everglades.
     d. No mistakes.

49.   **a.** Colds like many other viruses are highly contagious.
     b. Call me when you feel better.
     c. Did you wash your hands, Michael?
     d. No mistakes.

50.   **a.** The industrial revolution began in Europe.
     b. Is Labor Day a national holiday?
     c. General Patton was a four-star general.
     d. No mistakes.

51.   **a.** Carmen brought bread, and butter, and strawberry jam.
     b. Let's look at the map.
     c. Be sure to thank Aunt Helen for the gift.
     d. No mistakes.

52.   **a.** My Aunt Georgia loves to read Eighteenth-Century novels.
     b. Eli's sister's cousin lives in Alaska.
     c. Is that a German shepherd?
     d. No mistakes.

53.   **a.** Those shoes are too expensive.
     b. Michael's best friend is Patrick.
     c. Did you hear that Inez got a new puppy.
     d. No mistakes.

SET 5 (Answers begin on page 159.)

Questions 54–57 are based on the following passage. First, read the passage, and then choose the answer that shows the best capitalization and punctuation for each underlined part.

> Carol walked into the **(54)** <u>room switching</u> on the light as she entered. "Where is **(55)** <u>everybody?" she called</u>. She was about to leave when she heard **(56)** <u>giggling this</u> made her stop and listen more carefully. She threw open the closet door and found her **(57)** <u>friends they</u> were only playing a prank.

54. **a.** room; switching
  b. room. Switching
  c. room, switching
  d. room: switching
  e. correct as it is

55. **a.** everybody," she
  b. everybody." She
  c. everybody? she
  d. everybody"—she
  e. correct as it is

56. **a.** giggling; this
  b. giggling, this
  c. giggling:
  d. giggling? This
  e. correct as it is

57. **a.** friends, they
  b. friends—they
  c. friends? They
  d. friends! They
  e. correct as it is

Questions 58–61 are based on the following passage. First, read the passage, and then choose the answer that shows the best capitalization and punctuation for each underlined part.

June 2, 2006

Melanie Jeffords
312 Maple Avenue
Chicago, Illinois 60632

Mark (58) <u>Franklin, general manager</u>
Wholesome Food Market
1245 Main Street
Chicago, Illinois 60627

(59) <u>dear Mr. Franklin;</u>

I am writing to complain about the behavior of one of your sales clerks. On (60) <u>Monday May 22nd I</u> visited your store to return a package of ground turkey that I had purchased the day before. When I explained to your sales clerk that the expiration date on the package was May 1st, she was (61) <u>extremely rude and she</u> refused to refund my money. This is not the kind of treatment I expect from your fine establishment. I hope you will make restitution and have a discussion with your staff about customer service. My receipt is enclosed.

Sincerely yours,

Melaine Jeffords

58. a. Franklin, general Manager
  b. franklin, General Manager
  c. Franklin, General Manager
  d. Franklin, General manager
  e. correct as it is

59. a. Dear Mr. Franklin.
  b. Dear, Mr. franklin,
  c. dear Mr. Franklin:
  d. Dear Mr. Franklin:
  e. correct as it is

60. a. Monday, May 22nd I
    b. Monday May 22nd; I
    c. Monday. May 22nd I
    d. Monday, May 22nd, I
    e. correct as it is

61. a. extremely rude, and she
    b. extremely rude: and she
    c. extremely rude? And she
    d. extremely rude and, she
    e. correct as it is

NOUNS

Words that name a person, place, or thing. Some examples:

ca.	ma.	forest
ca.	tree	pen

Sentence Structure

A complete sentence requires two basic elements: a *subject* and a *predicate*. A predicate is a word or phrase that acts as a *verb*, describing action. A subject is generally a *noun*, describing who or what performed that action.

A complete sentence, therefore, might contain only two words, such as this: *You go!* In this example, *go* is the verb describing the action, and *you* is the subject performing that action. Here are some more examples:

The cat | is black.
subject | predicate

Mike | likes to eat.
subject | predicate

The tired students | rode the bus.
subject | predicate

Notice that the subjects and predicates in the previous examples might each be one word—the proper noun *Mike* forms one subject, and the verb *go* forms one predicate—but they are often composed of phrases rather than single words. The phrase *likes to eat* works together to form one predicate, while the phrase *the tired students* forms a subject.

The important thing to remember is that a sentence is not complete unless it contains both a predicate (the action being performed) and a subject (the person or thing performing that action). If the subject or predicate is missing, it is an incomplete sentence or *sentence fragment*.

Sentences, however, are generally not as short and direct as these examples; these are known as *simple sentences*, but most writing consists of *complex sentences*. Our simple sentences each consist of one *clause*, or one complete thought. Complex sentences, however, are made up of two or more *clauses*, or two or more ideas combined into a single sentence.

The sentence *Mike likes to eat* consists of one clause, one complete idea. The sentence *Mike likes to eat, but he isn't fat* contains two separate ideas, each contained in a separate clause. Some clauses can stand on their own as complete sentences, such as in our previous example: *Mike likes to eat. He isn't fat.* These are called *independent clauses*; an independent clause contains a subject (*he*) and a predicate (*isn't fat*). Clauses that could not form complete sentences are called *dependent clauses*, because they depend on another clause to make sense. Here is another example:

I'll help you on Thursday, | if possible.
independent clause | dependent clause

The first clause in that sentence is independent because it could stand on its own as a complete sentence: *I'll help you on Thursday*. The second clause, however, is *not* a complete sentence—*if possible*; it depends upon the first clause to make sense.

Here are some more terms that you'll need to understand:

✓ **Independent clause:** a clause that expresses a complete sentence. →*Monica walked on the grass.*
✓ **Dependent (subordinate) clause:** a clause that does not express a complete sentence. →*though it was wet*
  Monica walked on the grass, though it was wet.
✓ **Essential clause:** a dependent clause that is necessary to the basic meaning of the completed sentence. →*who are pregnant*
  Women who are pregnant can crave salty or sweet foods.
✓ **Nonessential clause:** a dependent clause that is not necessary to the basic meaning of the completed sentence. →*who growls whenever the phone rings*
  Elmo, who growls whenever the phone rings, tried to attack the vacuum cleaner.

✓ **Appositive:** a phrase that makes a preceding noun or pronoun clearer or more definite by explaining or identifying it.→*rice pudding and fruit salad Candice's grandfather brought her favorite desserts, rice pudding and fruit salad.*

✓ **Fragment:** a phrase punctuated like a sentence even though it does not express a complete thought.→*Timothy saw the car. And ran.*

✓ **Coordinating Conjunction:** a word that joins two independent and equal clauses. (*and, but, so, or, for, nor, yet*)→*Dorothy had a beautiful rose garden, and her yard was a profusion of color every summer.*

✓ **Subordinating Conjunction:** a word that makes a clause dependent (*after, although, as, because, before, if, once, since, than, that, though, unless, until, when, whenever, where, wherever, while*)→*The man wasn't angry, though he had a right to be.*

✓ **Conjunctive Adverb:** a word that introduces a relationship between two independent clauses (*accordingly, besides, consequently, furthermore, hence, however, instead, moreover, nevertheless, otherwise, then, therefore, thus*)→*On Tuesdays, I play racquetball; otherwise, I would go with you.* Conjuctive adverbs are generally preceded by a semicolon.

To construct a sentence:

✓ Begin with a subject (noun) and a predicate (verb).

✓ Always have at least one independent clause in the sentence.

✓ Join two independent clauses with a semicolon or a comma and a **conjunction.**→*Chaucer was a narrator, and he was a pilgrim in his* Canterbury Tales.

✓ Do not run two or more independent clauses together without punctuation; that error is appropriately called a **run-on**. Wrong: *Chaucer was a narrator and he was a pilgrim in his* Canterbury Tales.

✓ Do not separate two independent clauses with just a comma; that error is called a **comma splice**. Wrong: *Chaucer was a narrator, he was a pilgrim in his* Canterbury Tales.

✓ Do not use a **conjunctive adverb** (the words *accordingly, besides, consequently, furthermore, hence, however, instead, moreover, nevertheless, otherwise, then, therefore, thus*) like a **conjunction**. Wrong: *Chaucer was a narrator, moreover he was a pilgrim in his* Canterbury Tales.

✓ As a general rule, do not begin a sentence with a dependent clause. Wrong: *Although I was tired, I kept walking*. Right: *I kept walking, although I was tired*. This rule can be broken on occasion for stylistic effect, but in general, it should be followed.

✓ Use a comma after a conjunctive adverb when it follows a semicolon.

✓ Use commas around nonessential clauses. Do not use commas around essential clauses.

✓ Use commas around appositives.

✓ Use commas around parenthetical elements (a word or group of words that interrupt a sentence's flow).→*Mrs. Moses, that mean old crone, yelled at little Paula for laughing too loud.*

SET 6 (Answers begin on page 160.)

Fill in the blank with the word that creates the most logical sentence. (Hint: Use a dictionary to determine which words best complete the sentence's meaning.)

62. Bonnie did not go to her class reunion; _____ was simply not in the mood.
  a. but she
  b. whenever she
  c. although she
  d. she

63. Lila wasn't feeling well. _____, she decided to stay home from work.
  a. Therefore
  b. Meanwhile
  c. However
  d. Anyway

64. Dave loved to go fishing, _____ this time he was not enjoying himself.
  a. when
  b. but
  c. so
  d. because

65. Ruby loves blueberry pie _____ it is made with freshly picked blueberries.
  a. whether
  b. because
  c. when
  d. as if

66. Mitchell loves listening to jazz and rhythm and blues. Greg, _____, will only listen to country.
    a. however
    b. then
    c. too
    d. therefore

67. Please close the windows, _____ we have the heat on.
    a. but
    b. however
    c. therefore
    d. since

68. The ticket said that the show would start at 8:00, but the curtains didn't go up _____ 8:30.
    a. less than
    b. until
    c. about
    d. since

69. My neighbor is deathly afraid of dogs; _____, I never let my Golden Retriever, Sandy, outside without a leash.
    a. moreover
    b. yet
    c. mainly
    d. consequently

70. The wedding quilt was designed as a sentimental way to make use of fabric taken _____ blankets and bedding that belonged to older couples in her family.
    a. from
    b. with
    c. in
    d. at

71. Sandra Day O'Connor, the first woman to serve on the U.S. Supreme Court, _____ appointed by President Ronald Reagan in 1981.
 a. she
 b. and
 c. but
 d. was

72. I _____ the speech you gave last Thursday night, but I was in bed with the flu.
 a. will have heard
 b. would hear
 c. might hear
 d. would have heard

73. _____ the Beatles' most popular songs—most of which were written by Lennon and McCartney—are "I Want to Hold Your Hand" and "Hey Jude."
 a. With
 b. Considering
 c. Among
 d. To

PROPER NOUNS

The specific name or title of a particular person, place, or thing. Proper nouns are generally capitalized. Some examples:

George Washington	New York City
Jennifer Jones	the Empire State Building

SET 7 (Answers begin on page 161.)
Choose the sentence that best combines the underlined sentences.

74. The airport is called the Glynco Jetport. The airline reservations and travel systems refer to its location as Brunswick, Georgia.
    a. Where the airport is called the Glynco Jetport, the airline reservations and travel systems refer to the location as Brunswick, Georgia.
    b. But the airport is called the Glynco Jetport, the airline reservations and travel systems refer to the location as Brunswick, Georgia.
    c. Even though the airline reservations and travel systems refer to the location as Brunswick, Georgia, the airport is called the Glynco Jetport.
    d. When the airport is called the Glynco Jetport, the airline reservations refer to the location as Brunswick, Georgia, and the travel systems.

75. Plato believed that boys and girls should be given an equal education. This idea is rarely mentioned in textbooks.
    a. Plato believed that boys and girls should be given an equal education, where this idea is rarely mentioned in textbooks.
    b. Plato believed that boys and girls should be given an equal education, an idea that is rarely mentioned in textbooks.
    c. Believing that boys and girls should be given an equal education, Plato's idea is rarely mentioned in textbooks.
    d. Plato believed that boys and girls should be given an equal education, whereupon this idea is rarely mentioned in textbooks.

76. Recently there have been government cutbacks in funds. Experts foresee steady hiring in the government's future.
    a. Despite recent government cutbacks in funds, experts foresee steady hiring in the government's future.
    b. Whereupon recent government cutbacks in funds, experts foresee steady hiring in the government's future.
    c. So that there have been recent government cutbacks in funds, experts foresee steady hiring in the government's future.
    d. Nonetheless, there have been recent government cutbacks in funds, experts foresee steady hiring in the government's future.

77. The federal government has a diverse number of jobs and geographic locations. The federal government offers flexibility in job opportunities that is unmatched in the private sector.

    a. In spite of its diversity of jobs and geographic locations, the federal government offers flexibility in job opportunities that is unmatched in the private sector.

    b. No matter its diversity of jobs and geographic locations, the federal government offers flexibility in job opportunities that is unmatched in the private sector.

    c. Because of its diversity of jobs and geographic locations, the federal government offers flexibility in job opportunities that is unmatched in the private sector.

    d. The federal government has a diverse number of jobs and geographic locations, so it offers flexibility in job opportunities that is unmatched in the private sector.

78. The Greeks thought that the halcyon, or kingfisher, nested on the sea. All birds nest on land.

    a. Whereupon all birds nest on land, the Greeks thought that the halcyon, or kingfisher, nested on the sea.

    b. The Greeks thought that the halcyon, or kingfisher, nested on the sea, whereas all birds nest on land.

    c. Whenever all birds nest on land, the Greeks thought that the halcyon, or kingfisher, nested on the sea.

    d. The Greeks thought that the halcyon, or kingfisher, nested on the sea, as all birds nest on land.

79. My cat loves to sleep in the sun. She sleeps on the radiator when it's cloudy.

    a. Because it's cloudy, my cat sleeps in the sun or on the radiator.

    b. My cat loves to sleep in the sun, and she sleeps on the radiator when it's cloudy.

    c. My cat loves to sleep in the sun because, when it's cloudy, she sleeps on the radiator.

    d. When it's cloudy, my cat sleeps on the radiator; when it's sunny, she sleeps in the sun.

80. <u>The president spoke at great length. I still don't understand his</u>
<u>policies.</u>

   a. Although I don't understand his policies, the president spoke at
great length.

   b. At great length the president spoke; understand his policies I
do not.

   c. The president spoke at great length, yet I still don't understand
his policies.

   d. The president spoke at great length, therefore I still don't
understand his policies.

PRONOUNS

A word used in place of a noun, generally referring to something
or someone who has already been identified. *George said that*
he *would go. He* is a pronoun used in place of the proper noun
George, since George had already been identified as the subject
of the sentence. Some common pronouns:

he	she	it
his	her	its
they	their	our

---

81. <u>The wisdom of the hedgehog is applauded in medieval bestiaries.</u>
<u>The hedgehog builds a nest with two exits and, when in danger,</u>
<u>rolls itself into a prickly ball.</u>

   a. The wisdom of the hedgehog is applauded in medieval bestiaries, while the hedgehog builds a nest with two exits and, when
in danger, rolls itself into a prickly ball.

   b. The hedgehog builds a nest with two exits and, when in danger, rolls itself into a prickly ball, so its wisdom is applauded in
medieval bestiaries.

   c. The hedgehog builds a nest with two exits and, when in danger,
rolls itself into a prickly ball, but its wisdom is applauded in
medieval bestiaries.

   d. Its wisdom applauded in medieval bestiaries, the hedgehog
builds a nest with two exits and, when in danger, rolls itself into
a prickly ball

82. <u>I just bought a new car. My old one died.</u>
   a. I just bought a new car, although my old one died.
   b. While I just bought a new car, my old one died.
   c. Because I just bought a new car, my old one died.
   d. I just bought a new car because my old one died.

83. <u>Most species of the bacterium Streptococcus are harmless. Some</u>
   <u>species of Streptococcus are dangerous pathogens.</u>
   a. Whereas most species of the bacterium Streptococcus are
   harmless, some are dangerous pathogens.
   b. Since most species of the bacterium Streptococcus are harmless,
   some are dangerous pathogens.
   c. As most species of the bacterium Streptococcus are harmless,
   some are dangerous pathogens.
   d. Because most species of the bacterium Streptococcus are harmless, some are dangerous pathogens.

84. <u>The man nodded politely. His expression was bewildered.</u>
   a. Nodding politely, the man's expression was bewildered.
   b. The man nodded politely his expression was bewildered.
   c. The man nodded politely, his expression bewildered.
   d. The man nodded politely, since his expression was bewildered.

SUBJECT AND PREDICATE NOUNS

Predicate = The action being performed.

Subject = Who or what performed the action.

Example:

    George | ate fish.

    subject | *predicate*

SET 8 (Answers begin on page 162.)
Choose the sentence that best combines the underlined sentences.

85. <u>Watching a TV show is a passive behavior. Playing a computer game is an interactive one.</u>
   a. Watching a TV show is a passive behavior, or playing a computer game is an interactive one.
   b. Watching a TV show is a passive behavior, for playing a computer game is an interactive one.
   c. Watching a TV show is a passive behavior, but playing a computer game is an interactive one.
   d. Being that playing a computer game is an interactive one, watching a TV show is a passive behavior.

86. <u>Socrates taught that we should question everything, even the law. He was both greatly loved and profoundly hated.</u>
   a. That he was both greatly loved and profoundly hated, Socrates taught that we should question everything, even the law.
   b. Socrates taught that we should question everything, even the law, so he was both greatly loved and profoundly hated.
   c. Socrates taught that we should question everything, even the law, which he was both greatly loved and profoundly hated.
   d. Socrates taught that we should question everything, even the law, for he was both greatly loved and profoundly hated.

87. <u>Sailors are said to catch albatrosses with baited hooks let down into the ship's wake. To kill the albatross was thought to be bad luck, so they were released immediately.</u>
   a. Sailors are said to catch albatrosses with baited hooks let down into the ship's wake, then release them again, for to kill the albatross was thought to be bad luck.
   b. With baited hooks let down into the ship's wake, sailors are said to catch albatrosses then release them again, so to kill the albatross was thought to be bad luck.
   c. Sailors are said to catch albatrosses with baited hooks let down into the ship's wake, then release them again, or to kill the albatross was thought to be bad luck.
   d. To kill the albatross was thought to be bad luck, so sailors are said to catch albatrosses with baited hooks let down into the ship's wake, only to release them immediately.

88. The symptoms of diabetes often develop gradually and are hard to identify at first. Nearly half of all people with diabetes do not know they have it.

a. The symptoms of diabetes often develop gradually and are hard to identify at first, so nearly half of all people with diabetes do not know they have it.

b. The symptoms of diabetes often develop gradually and are hard to identify at first, yet nearly half of all people with diabetes do not know they have it.

c. Nearly half of all people with diabetes do not know they have it, and the symptoms of diabetes often develop gradually and are hard to identify at first.

d. The symptoms of diabetes often develop gradually for nearly half of all people with diabetes do not know they have it and are hard to identify at first.

89. The French philosopher Voltaire was greatly respected. Voltaire spent almost a year imprisoned in the Bastille.

a. The French philosopher Voltaire was greatly respected, so he spent almost a year imprisoned in the Bastille.

b. The French philosopher Voltaire was greatly respected with almost a year imprisoned in the Bastille.

c. The French philosopher Voltaire was greatly respected, or he spent almost a year imprisoned in the Bastille.

d. The French philosopher Voltaire was greatly respected, yet he spent almost a year imprisoned in the Bastille.

90. I don't understand why she was angry. I explained why I was late.

a. I don't understand why she was angry, whereas I explained why I was late.

b. While I don't understand why she is angry, I therefore explained why I was late.

c. I don't understand why she was angry, because I explained why I was late.

d. When I explained why I was late, I don't understand why she was angry.

91. Sylvia is loaded with money. She can afford that trip to Silver Dollar City.

    a. Sylvia is loaded with money, or she can afford that trip to Silver Dollar City.

    b. Sylvia is loaded with money, but she can afford that trip to Silver Dollar City.

    c. Sylvia is loaded with money, so she can afford that trip to Silver Dollar City.

    d. Sylvia is loaded with money, yet she can afford that trip to Silver Dollar City.

92. The rules of statistics say that it is possible for all the air in a room to move to one corner. This is extremely unlikely.

    a. The rules of statistics say that it is possible for all the air in a room to move to one corner, or this is extremely unlikely.

    b. The rules of statistics say that it is possible for all the air in a room to move to one corner, but this is extremely unlikely.

    c. This is extremely unlikely in that the rules of statistics say that it is possible for all the air in a room to move to one corner.

    d. For all the air in a room to move to one corner, this is extremely unlikely, according to the rules of statistics saying that it is possible.

93. Will you come on Thursday? And will you bring some ice?

    a. Will you come on Thursday, or bring some ice?

    b. On Thursday, when you come, bring ice.

    c. Will you come on Thursday, and bring some ice?

    d. Will you come on Thursday; bring ice.

94. Bats are not rodents. Bats bear a surface resemblance to a winged mouse.

    a. Bats are not rodents, although they do bear a resemblance to a winged mouse.

    b. Bats are not rodents that they bear a surface resemblance to a winged mouse.

    c. Bats are not rodents, when they bear a surface resemblance to a winged mouse.

    d. Bats are not rodents, if they bear a surface resemblance to a winged mouse.

95. <u>Art is not only found in the museum or concert hall. Art can be found in the expressive behavior of ordinary people, as well.</u>

    a. Art can be found not only in the museum or concert hall, and it can be found in the expressive behavior of ordinary people, as well.

    b. In the museum or concert hall, art can be found not only there and in the expressive behavior of ordinary people, as well.

    c. Although in the expressive behavior of ordinary people, as well, art can be found not only in the museum or concert hall.

    d. Art can be found not only in the museum or concert hall, but in the expressive behavior of ordinary people, as well.

96. <u>The new store is open for business. You wouldn't know it.</u>

    a. The new store is open—you wouldn't know it for business.

    b. Because the new store is open for business, you wouldn't know it.

    c. Although you wouldn't know it, the new store is open for business.

    d. The new store is open for business, although you wouldn't know it.

SET 9 (Answers begin on page 163.)
Choose the sentence that best combines the underlined sentences.

97. <u>My favorite color is blue. I have no blue shirts.</u>

    a. Blue, being my favorite color, I have no blue shirts.

    b. I have no blue shirts because blue is my favorite color.

    c. My favorite color is blue, since I have no blue shirts.

    d. My favorite color is blue, yet I have no blue shirts.

98. <u>Polly is very conceited. Polly is bright.</u>

    a. Polly is very conceited, whereas Polly is bright.

    b. Polly is bright, but she is very conceited.

    c. Being bright, Polly is conceited.

    d. If Polly is conceited, she must be bright.

99. <u>Yesterday was Thursday. Tomorrow must be Saturday.</u>

    a. As tomorrow is Saturday, yesterday must be Thursday.

    b. Yesterday was Thursday, whereas tomorrow must be Saturday.

    c. Yesterday was Thursday, so tomorrow must be Saturday.

    d. Since yesterday was Thursday, tomorrow must be Saturday.

100. <u>This neighborhood is called "baby central." Almost every family</u>
<u>within a three-block radius has a child under the age of one.</u>
   a. Almost every family within a three-block radius has a child under
   the age of one, while this neighborhood is called "baby central."
   b. Almost every family within a three-block radius has a child under
   the age of one, but this neighborhood is called "baby central."
   c. Almost every family within a three-block radius has a child
   under the age of one; therefore, this neighborhood is called
   "baby central."
   d. This neighborhood is called "baby central:" meanwhile, almost
   every family within a three-block radius has a child under the
   age of one.

101. <u>The new shopping mall has 200 stores. The new shopping mall</u>
<u>doesn't have a pet shop.</u>
   a. The new shopping mall has 200 stores; however, it doesn't have
   a pet shop.
   b. Instead of a pet shop, the new shopping mall has 200 stores.
   c. With 200 stores, the new shopping mall doesn't have a pet shop.
   d. The new shopping mall has 200 stores, and it doesn't have a
   pet shop.

102. <u>Eugene has a difficult personality. Eugene is unreliable.</u>
   a. Eugene has a difficult personality, and furthermore he's
   unreliable.
   b. Eugene has a difficult personality, although he is unreliable.
   c. While he is unreliable, Eugene has a difficult personality.
   d. Being unreliable, Eugene has a difficult personality.

103. <u>We never eat candy or ice cream. We do drink soda.</u>
   a. We never eat candy or ice cream, but we do drink soda.
   b. Because we never eat candy or ice cream, we drink soda.
   c. We never eat candy or ice cream, so we do drink soda.
   d. We never eat candy or ice cream and drink soda.

104. Having several cavities filled during a dental appointment is definitely unpleasant. It is not as unpleasant as having a root canal.

a. Having several cavities filled during a dental appointment is definitely unpleasant, so it is not as unpleasant as having a root canal.

b. Having several cavities filled during a dental appointment is definitely unpleasant, and it is not as unpleasant as having a root canal.

c. Having several cavities filled during a dental appointment is definitely unpleasant, but it is not as unpleasant as having a root canal.

d. Having several cavities filled during a dental appointment is definitely unpleasant, or it is not as unpleasant as having a root canal.

105. She loves celebrating her birthday. She always has a big party.

a. She loves celebrating her birthday, to where she always has a big party.

b. Although she loves celebrating her birthday, she always has a big party.

c. She always has a big party, meanwhile she loves celebrating her birthday.

d. She loves celebrating her birthday, so she always has a big party.

106. Insomnia is not usually a physical problem. It can affect one's physical health.

a. Insomnia is not usually a physical problem; therefore, it can affect one's physical health.

b. Insomnia is not usually a physical problem, yet it can affect one's physical health.

c. Insomnia not usually a physical problem can affect one's physical health.

d. Insomnia is not usually a physical problem, so it can affect one's physical health.

107. True narcolepsy is the sudden and irresistible onset of sleep during waking hours. True narcolepsy is extremely dangerous.
   a. While true narcolepsy is the sudden and irresistible onset of sleep during waking hours and is extremely dangerous.
   b. The sudden and irresistible onset of sleep during waking hours, which is true narcolepsy but extremely dangerous.
   c. True narcolepsy is the sudden and irresistible onset of sleep during waking hours, yet narcolepsy is extremely dangerous.
   d. True narcolepsy is the sudden and irresistible onset of sleep during waking hours, and it is extremely dangerous.

108. There has been much interest in dreams throughout the ages. The empirical, scientific study of dreams is relatively new.
   a. Despite much interest in dreams throughout the ages, the empirical, scientific study of dreams being relatively new.
   b. There has been much interest in dreams throughout the ages, yet the empirical, scientific study of dreams is relatively new.
   c. While much interest in dreams throughout the ages, although the empirical, scientific study of dreams is relatively new.
   d. There has been much interest in dreams throughout the ages, for the empirical, scientific study of dreams is relatively new.

SET 10 (Answers begin on page 164.)
Replace the underlined portion with the phrase that best completes the sentence. Choose **a** if the sentence is correct as is.

109. I look forward to welcoming you and having the opportunity to show you around our office.
   a. I look forward to welcoming you and having
   b. I will look forward to our welcome and having
   c. As I look forward to welcoming you and to have
   d. I look forward to welcoming you and have
   e. Looking forward to welcoming you and hoping to have

110. <u>Although she was not supposed to, Megan went to the party.</u>
   a. Although she was not supposed to, Megan went to the party.
   b. Although Megan went to the party, she was not supposed to.
   c. Megan went to the party, even though she was not supposed to.
   d. When Megan was not supposed to, she went to the party.
   e. Since she was not supposed to, Megan went to the party.

111. The steak was cooked <u>properly however</u>, it was still tough.
   a. properly however,
   b. properly; however,
   c. properly, however,
   d. properly, however;
   e. properly however

112. Most of a human tooth is made up of a substance known as <u>dentin, which is located</u> directly below the enamel.
   a. dentin, which is located
   b. dentin, and which is located
   c. dentin but located
   d. dentin, which it is located
   e. dentin, that its location is

113. Jackson Pollock, <u>a twentieth-century American painter, is well known and renowned for creating</u> abstract paintings by dripping paint on canvas.
   a. a twentieth-century American painter, is well known and renowned for creating
   b. an American painter who lived and painted in the twentieth century, is well known for the creation of
   c. renowned and prominent, was known as a twentieth-century American painter for creating
   d. he is an American painter famous and renowned for creating
   e. a twentieth-century American painter, is famous for creating

114. Mark ran the course in record <u>time he</u> is the best runner on the team.
 a. time he
 b. time, he
 c. time; he
 d. time: he
 e. time? He

115. This test will affect your final <u>grade; therefore,</u> do your very best.
 a. grade; therefore,
 b. grade therefore,
 c. grade, therefore,
 d. grade, therefore;
 e. grade therefore

116. The <u>dog growling fiercely</u> came toward me.
 a. dog growling fiercely
 b. dog, growling fiercely
 c. dog: growling fiercely,
 d. dog, growling fiercely,
 e. dog growling fiercely;

117. Baseball is a sport that is <u>popular in the United States like Japan.</u>
 a. popular in the United States like Japan.
 b. as well popular in Japan as it is in the United States
 c. just as popular in the United States than in Japan
 d. popular in the United States as well as in Japan.
 e. popular as well as in both Japan and the United States

118. I decided to paint the kitchen <u>yellow, and after I had painted, my husband</u> informed me that he'd prefer blue.
 a. yellow, and after I had painted, my husband
 b. yellow, and after I had painted my husband
 c. yellow and after I had painted, my husband
 d. yellow; and, after I had painted, my husband
 e. yellow and after I had painted my husband

119. <u>Yelling after it as the taxi drove away, leaving Austin and me standing helplessly on the sidewalk.</u>

    a. Yelling after it as the taxi drove away, leaving Austin and me standing helplessly on the sidewalk.

    b. While yelling after it and watching the taxi drive away, which left Austin and me standing helplessly on the sidewalk.

    c. Left helplessly standing on the sidewalk after Austin and me yelled after the taxi and watched as it drove away.

    d. The taxi drove away as we yelled after it, leaving Austin and me standing helplessly on the sidewalk.

    e. After having yelled after it, the taxi driving off and leaving Austin and me on the sidewalk, watching helplessly.

INDEPENDENT CLAUSE

A portion of a sentence that contains a subject and a predicate. An independent clause could stand alone as a complete sentence. Example:

    I worked yesterday, | and I will again tomorrow.

    independent clause | *independent clause*

SET 11 (Answers begin on page 165.)

Replace the underlined portion with the phrase that best completes the sentence. Choose **a** if the sentence is correct as is.

120. When making a chocolate torte, <u>only the best ingredients should be used.</u>

    a. only the best ingredients should be used.

    b. you should use only the best ingredients.

    c. the best ingredients only should be used.

    d. one should have used only the best ingredients.

    e. using only the best ingredients is essential.

121. It was the front tire, <u>rather than the rear, which</u> hit the curb.
   a. rather than the rear, which
   b. rather than the rear; which,
   c. which, rather than the rear,
   d. rather than the rear which
   e. rather than the rear which,

122. This was the fifth <u>of the five speeches that the mayor gave during</u> <u>this the month of May.</u>
   a. This was the fifth of the five speeches the mayor gave during this the month of May.
   b. Of the five speeches the mayor gave during May, this was the fifth one.
   c. Thus far during the month of May, the mayor gave five speeches and this was the fifth.
   d. This fifth speech of the mayor's given during the month of May was one of five speeches.
   e. This was the fifth speech the mayor has given during the month of May.

123. Mark Twain's <u>book *Roughing It* describes</u> his travels as a young man.
   a. book *Roughing It* describes
   b. book; *Roughing It*
   c. book *Roughing It* describe's
   d. book; *Roughing It* describes
   e. book, *Roughing It*, describes

124. We loved our trip to the <u>desert where you could see</u> the tall cactus, the blooming flowers, and the little desert animals.
   a. desert where you could see
   b. desert; you could see
   c. desert; where we saw
   d. desert; we saw
   e. desert in that you saw

125. The stock market rose by 22 points this month, <u>opposite in what</u> <u>many financial analysts had predicted</u>.
  a. opposite in what many financial analysts had predicted.
  b. contrary to the predictions of many financial analysts.
  c. as against the predictions of many financial analysts.
  d. contrasting of many financial analysts' predictions.
  e. contrary with what many financial analysts predicted.

126. A standardized extract made from the leaves of the ginkgo biloba tree <u>is proving to be effective in treating</u> mild to moderate Alzheimer's disease.
  a. is proving to be effective in treating
  b. has shown its proof of effectiveness with treating
  c. may have proven effective treatment for
  d. is effectively proving in treating
  e. have given a proven effectiveness in the treatment of

127. The citizens' action committee has accused the city counsel members <u>with being careless with the spending of</u> the taxpayers' money.
  a. with being careless with the spending of
  b. as to carelessness in the spending of
  c. of carelessness in the spending of
  d. of careless spending to
  e. with spending carelessly of

128. Aspirin was exclusively known <u>as a painkiller until the time when</u> <u>cardiologists began prescribing it as a preventive for</u> heart attacks.
  a. as a painkiller until the time when cardiologists began prescribing it as a preventive for
  b. to be a painkiller since when cardiologists prescribed it to be a prevention for
  c. as a way to kill and stop pain until cardiologists began to prescribe it as a method for the prevention of
  d. as a painkiller until cardiologists began prescribing it as a preventive for
  e. to be a painkiller up to when cardiologists prescribed its preventive for

129. The news reporter who <u>had been covering the story suddenly be-</u>
<u>came ill, and I was called</u> to take her place.
  a. had been covering the story suddenly became ill, and I was called
  b. was covering the story suddenly becomes ill, and they called me
  c. is covering the story suddenly becomes ill, and I was called
  d. would have been covering the story suddenly became ill, and I
    am called
  e. covers the story, suddenly became ill, and they called me

130. <u>Donald Trump, the son of a real estate developer, he</u> has built a
billion-dollar empire.
  a. Donald Trump, the son of a real estate developer, he
  b. Donald Trump, being the son of a real estate developer,
  c. While he was the son of a real estate developer, Donald Trump
  d. The son of a real estate developer, Donald Trump
  e. Donald Trump, the son of a real estate developer, and he

131. The troposphere is the lowest layer of Earth's <u>atmosphere, it ex-</u>
<u>tends</u> from ground level to an altitude of seven to ten miles.
  a. atmosphere, it extends
  b. atmosphere of which it extends
  c. atmosphere. Extending
  d. atmosphere, and extending
  e. atmosphere; it extends

132. <u>While they may be colorful, many snakes are very dangerous.</u>
  a. While they may be colorful, many snakes are very dangerous.
  b. Many snakes are very dangerous, even if they are colorful.
  c. While they are very dangerous, many snakes are colorful.
  d. While they may be colorful; many snakes are very dangerous.
  e. While they may be dangerous. Many snakes are colorful.

133. <u>Our contention is that a body of common knowledge shared by</u> lit-
erate Americans of the late twentieth century and that this knowledge can be defined.
  a. Our contention is that a body of common knowledge shared by
  b. To contend that a body of common knowledge is shared by
  c. We contend that we share a body of common knowledge in
  d. That a common body of knowledge is shared is our contention with
  e. It is our contention that a body of common knowledge is shared by

134. <u>Whether they earn</u> a BS degree, chemical engineers are almost guaranteed a job.
   a. Whether they earn
   b. If they earn
   c. If earning
   d. To earn
   e. Since earning

SET 12 (Answers begin on page 166.)
Choose the sentence that is NOT correctly written or that is unclear. Choose choice **d** if all sentences are correct.

135. **a.** We asked him to pick us up in the morning.
   b. Mrs. Jacobs needed a ride to the airport.
   c. The car racing up the street.
   d. No mistakes.

136. **a.** Our neighbors went on vacation; going to the Grand Canyon.
   b. There are yellow and red tulips in my garden.
   c. We invited Molly to our house for dinner.
   d. No mistakes.

137. **a.** We are planning to build a new fence in our backyard.
   b. Where is the new diner that everyone is talking about?
   c. There's nothing I can do to help.
   d. No mistakes.

138. **a.** Make sure the door is locked.
   b. I love pumpkin pie Pearl does too.
   c. Yes, I will bring the dessert.
   d. No mistakes.

139. **a.** After he left, I went straight to bed.
   b. For the first time, I understood what she was talking about.
   c. We visited the town where my father grew up last summer.
   d. No mistakes.

140. **a.** Kate was allergic to all dairy products.
    b. Which of the Beatles' songs is your favorite?
    c. The company newsletter explained the new vacation policy.
    d. No mistakes.

141. **a.** They went to the park and flew a kite.
    b. "Don't tell me what to do," she shouted.
    c. Liam loves the warm weather, unless he knows it won't last much longer.
    d. No mistakes.

142. **a.** Bring your umbrella tomorrow it's supposed to rain.
    b. The dancers' costumes were being delivered on Saturday.
    c. Would you consider taking me as your guest?
    d. No mistakes.

143. **a.** Marlene likes my apple crisp better than Aunt Kate's.
    b. The people in the auditorium, whether they were seated or standing.
    c. I registered for a class in West Indian literature.
    d. No mistakes.

144. **a.** The free passes were given to Lena and me.
    b. Where's my purple umbrella?
    c. After midnight, the light on the front porch goes off.
    d. No mistakes.

145. **a.** Katya and I were in the same pottery class.
    b. The weather was nicer today than it was yesterday.
    c. The grapes cost more than the melon does.
    d. No mistakes.

146. **a.** His jacket is just like mine.
    b. Talia went to yoga class, and that she forgot her mat.
    c. Indira visits her relatives frequently.
    d. No mistakes.

SET 13 (Answers begin on page 167.)
Choose the sentence that expresses the idea most clearly.

147. **a.** For three weeks, the Merryville Fire Chief received taunting calls from an arsonist, who would not say where he intended to set the next fire.
   b. The Merryville Fire Chief received taunting calls from an arsonist, but he would not say where he intended to set the next fire, for three weeks.
   c. He would not say where he intended to set the next fire, but for three weeks the Merryville Fire Chief received taunting calls from an arsonist.
   d. The Merryville Fire Chief received taunting calls from an arsonist for three weeks, not saying where he intended to set the next fire.

148. **a.** There is no true relationship between ethics and the law.
   b. Ethics and the law having no true relationship.
   c. Between ethics and the law, no true relationship.
   d. Ethics and the law is no true relationship.

149. **a.** Some people say jury duty is a nuisance that just takes up their precious time and that we don't get paid enough.
   b. Some people say jury duty is a nuisance that just takes up your precious time and that one doesn't get paid enough.
   c. Some people say jury duty is a nuisance that just takes up precious time and that doesn't pay enough.
   d. Some people say jury duty is a nuisance that just takes up our precious time and that they don't get paid enough.

150. **a.** The mayor told the residents to evacuate the city as soon as possible.
   b. As soon as possible, the mayor told the residents to evacuate the city.
   c. To evacuate the city as soon as possible, the mayor told the residents.
   d. "Evacuate the city," the mayor told the residents as soon as possible.

151. **a.** A sharpshooter for many years, Miles Johnson could hit the bull's-eye every time.
   b. Miles Johnson had been a sharpshooter for many years, and he could hit the bull's-eye every time.
   c. Hitting the bull's-eye every time, Miles Johnson had been a sharpshooter for many years.
   d. Because he could hit the bull's-eye every time, he had been a sharpshooter for many years.

152. **a.** By the time they are in the third or fourth grade, the eyes of most children in the United States are tested.
   b. Most children by the time they are in the United States have their eyes tested in the third or fourth grade.
   c. Most children in the United States have their eyes tested by the time they are in the third or fourth grade.
   d. In the United States by the time of third or fourth grade, there is testing of the eyes of most children.

153. **a.** Ultraviolet radiation levels are 60% higher at 8,500 feet from the Sun than they are at sea level, according to researchers.
   b. Researchers have found from the Sun ultraviolet radiation levels 60% higher, they say, at 8,500 feet than at sea level.
   c. Researchers have found that ultraviolet radiation levels from the Sun are 60% higher at 8,500 feet than they are at sea level.
   d. At 8,500 feet researchers have found that ultraviolet radiation levels are 60% higher from sea level with the Sun's rays.

DEPENDENT CLAUSE

A portion of a sentence that cannot stand on its own as a complete sentence; it is *dependent* on the rest of the sentence to make sense. Example:

It's supposed to rain today, | unlike yesterday.

independent clause | *dependent clause*

Agreement

Agreement is a very important step in constructing a coherent sentence. There are three basic agreements in a sentence: subject-verb agreement, tense agreement, and antecedent-pronoun agreement.

First, you have to know the definition of a verb:
✓ **Verb**: a word or group of words describing the action or the state of being of a subject.

Subject-Verb Agreement

✓ If the subject is singular, the verb is singular; if the subject is plural, the verb is plural→*Mrs. Hendrickson feeds the birds every day.* Or: *The Hendricksons feed the birds every day.*
✓ Subjects joined by *and* are plural and receive a plural verb→*Jolie and Lara swim together every Thursday.*
✓ Subjects joined by *or* or *nor* adopt the singularity or plurality of the last subject; accordingly, the verb matches it→*Either that cat or those dogs have been eating my snacks!*

Pronoun-Antecedent Agreement

✓ *Each, either, neither, anybody, anyone, everybody, everyone, no one, nobody, one, somebody*, and *someone* are singular pronouns and receive singular verbs.→*Each of us is accountable for his own actions.*

✓ *Both, few, many*, and *several* are plural pronouns and receive plural verbs. →*Both of us are accountable.*

✓ *All, any, most, none*, and *some* can be singular or plural pronouns, depending on their use. These pronouns can receive plural or singular verbs.

✓ Sometimes a specific member (singular) of a larger group (plural) is the subject of a sentence. In that case, the verb would be singular rather than plural.→*One of the chairs is broken.* (The group of chairs is actually not broken, only one of them is—so the verb is singular.)

  →*The greatest of all the generals was George Washington.* (There were many generals, but the sentence specifically refers to George Washington.)

✓ Do not use *they, them*, or *their* in place of the pronouns, *he, him*, or *his*.→Incorrect: *Each student should check their own work.* Correct: *Each student should check his or her own work.*

Tense Agreement

✓ Maintain one tense in a complete thought: past tense or present tense.→ Incorrect: *In the game of hide and seek, Bobby chased Mary and tag her from behind.*
Correct: *In the game of hide and seek, Bobby chased Mary and tagged her from behind.*
Incorrect: *Dusk had just settled when I see a fawn timidly step onto the beach.*
Correct: *Dusk had just settled when I saw a fawn timidly step onto the beach.*

Do not use *of* in place of *have*.

You cannot avoid pronouns. *Pronouns* substitute for nouns. Instead of saying, "Because Janie was late, Janie hopped on Janie's moped, and Janie raced to the wedding," you would say, "Because Janie was late, *she* hopped on *her* moped, and *she* raced to the wedding."

  In this section, you will clarify ambiguous pronouns and assure pronoun-antecedent agreement, and you will also grapple with contractions. All too often, certain pronouns and contractions are confused. "The file cabinet drawer snagged on an overstuffed folder; *it's* now stuck just before *its* halfway point." *It's* is a contraction meaning *it is*, while *its* is a possessive pronoun meaning the drawer's halfway point. The only visual difference between the two is an apostrophe neatly inserted between the *t* and the *s* in the contraction.

Do You Know These Terms?

✓ **Antecedent**: In the last example, Janie is the specific noun that *she* and *her* replace; so Janie is the *antecedent*. The presence of the antecedent in a sentence is as important as which pronouns substitute for it.

✓ **Contractions**: Two words made into one by omitting letters and using an apostrophe to highlight the omission creates a contraction.

✓ **Subjective, Objective, and Possessive Cases**: Persons or things (nouns) acting on other things are subjects. Pronouns that refer to these subjects are in the subjective case (*I, you, he, she, we, they, who*). Persons or things acted upon (in other words, they are not performing the action) are objects. Pronouns that refer to these objects are in the objective case (*me, you, him, her, us, them, whom*). Subjects or objects that claim ownership of something are possessors. Pronouns that claim their possessions are in the possessive case (*my, your, his, her, our, your, whose*).

✓ **Avoid Ambiguous Pronoun References.** The antecedent that a pronoun refers to must be clearly stated and in close proximity to its pronoun.
    If more subjects than one are present, indicate which subject is the antecedent.→*When Katherine and Melissa left for England, she promised to write me about all their adventures.* Who is *she*? Katherine or Melissa?

Pronouns should

✓ Agree in number with their antecedent: Singular antecedents use singular pronouns, and plural antecedents use plural pronouns.

✓ *Compound antecedents* joined by *and* use plural pronouns.→*A horse and a donkey make a mule.* The horse and the donkey are singular subjects, but together they create one plural subject.

✓ *Compound antecedents* joined by *or* or *nor* use pronouns that agree with the nearest antecedent.→*Neither my one cat nor my four dogs are as difficult to maintain as my one pet fish.*

✓ *Collective nouns* use singular pronouns unless it is obvious that each person or thing in the group acts individually.→*The company mandated a universal naptime for all its employees. The company* is a group of many people, but in the first sentence the group is acting as a single entity, so the pronoun (*its*) is singular.

✓ Persons receive the pronouns *who, whom,* or *whose,* not *that* or *which.*

✓ After *is, are, was,* or *were,* use the subjective case.

✓ Pronouns preceding or following *infinitive verbs* (the plain form of a verb preceded by *to*) take the objective case.→*Billy Jean begged him to play catch, but he did not want to play ball with her at that moment.* In the first clause, *him* is the subject; in the second clause, *her* is an object. Despite their difference, both take the objective case because of the infinitive *to play.*

SET 14 (Answers begin on page 167.)
For the following questions, choose the underlined part of the sentence that contains a grammatical error. Choose answer **e** if there are no errors.

154. We knew that Lawrence must <u>of missed</u> the <u>appointment because</u>
                                                              a   b
train service <u>was disrupted</u> for three hours <u>this morning</u>. <u>No error.</u>
                              c   d   e

155. Every year, <u>a few committed</u> citizens <u>exceeds</u> our <u>expectations and</u>
                                           a   b   c
work tirelessly <u>to improve</u> our community programs in significant
                              d
ways. <u>No error.</u>
              e

156. <u>Each of</u> the employees <u>have had</u> a <u>half-hour</u> evaluation meeting
              a   b   c
<u>with</u> his or her supervisor. <u>No error.</u>
    d   e

157. Here <u>are</u> one of the three <u>keys</u> that you <u>will need</u> to unlock the office
                    a   b   c
door <u>tomorrow</u>. <u>No error.</u>
              d   e

158. <u>One of</u> the <u>students</u> <u>forgot</u> <u>their</u> books. <u>No error.</u>
              a   b   c   d   e

159. <u>Someone from</u> the garage phoned <u>to say</u> <u>that</u> the car had been
　　　　　a　　　　　　　　　　　　　　　　b　　c

fixed and <u>asking</u> if we would pick it up by 5:00. <u>No error.</u>
　　　　　　d　　　　　　　　　　　　　　　　　　　　　　e

160. The child <u>walked</u> into the <u>store</u>, expecting to <u>see</u> <u>their</u> cousin.
　　　　　　　　　　a　　　　　　　b　　　　　　　　　　c　　d

<u>No error.</u>
　e

161. The staff at the <u>university</u> library <u>deserve</u> recognition for <u>helping</u>
　　　　　　　　　　　　　a　　　　　　　b

<u>to locate</u> the <u>many sources needed</u> for the successful completion of
　c　　　　　　　d

my doctoral dissertation. <u>No error.</u>
　　　　　　　　　　　　　　　e

162. Diana <u>learned</u> to <u>swim</u>, <u>water ski,</u> and <u>to hike</u> at summer camp.
　　　　　　　a　　　　　b　　　　c　　　　　　　d

<u>No error.</u>
　e

163. <u>During</u> the winter season, homeowners should change <u>their</u>
　　　　　a　　　　　　　　　　　　　　　　　　　　　　　　　　　b

disposable furnace filters at least once <u>a month; a</u> dirty filter <u>reduce</u>
　　　　　　　　　　　　　　　　　　　　　　c　　　　　　　　　　d

furnace efficiency. <u>No error.</u>
　　　　　　　　　　e

164. The chief executive <u>officer and</u> the chairman of the board <u>agrees</u>
　　　　　　　　　　　　　　a　　　　　　　　　　　　　　　　　　　b

that the new benefit package <u>should include</u> a dental health plan
　　　　　　　　　　　　　　　　c

<u>as well as</u> eye care. <u>No error.</u>
　d　　　　　　　　e

165. Fred <u>watched</u> the game, but <u>begun</u> to <u>wonder</u> why he <u>cared</u> who won.
　　　　　　a　　　　　　　　　　b　　　　c　　　　　　　d

<u>No error.</u>
　e

SET 15 (Answers begin on page 168.)
Fill in the blank with the correct verb form.

166. On March 15, 2006, the Maywood Recreation Department requested a grant from the state to rebuild the community center
that _____ in the recent fire.
a. destroys
b. will be destroyed
c. had been destroyed
d. is being destroyed

167. Matthew Morris and Jessica Glassman hosted a holiday party that
The River Bank Café _____.
a. caters
b. will cater
c. is catering
d. catered

168. Megan is trying to read all three books in the series before summer
_____.
a. ended
b. will have ended
c. will end
d. ends

169. We have _____ more sweets since that wonderful bakery
opened down the block.
a. ate
b. been eating
c. been eat
d. eat

170. The plumber discovered a bad leak while _____ the sink.
a. repair
b. repaired
c. repairing
d. have repaired

171. Do not _____ until I blow the whistle.
   a. begin
   b. began
   c. begun
   d. beginning

172. It's after 2 P.M., so Ted _____ started by now.
   a. won't
   b. did not
   c. was
   d. should have

173. I hope _____ German someday.
   a. learn
   b. learned
   c. to learn
   d. learning

174. The woman who confronted the owner of the unleashed dog
   _____ angry.
   a. were
   b. was
   c. are
   d. have been

175. The boy _____ the bat and ran to first base as fast as he
   could.
   a. swings
   b. swinged
   c. swung
   d. swing

176. There _____ four excellent restaurants in the center of
   town.
   a. is
   b. are
   c. was
   d. being

177. The noise from the lawn mowers _____ louder as the morning progresses.
    a. gets
    b. get
    c. have gotten
    d. are getting

SET 16 (Answers begin on page 169.)
Replace the underlined words with the phrase that best completes the sentence. Choose **a** if the sentence is correct as is.

178. The words Equal Justice Under Law <u>is carved</u> above the main entrance to the Supreme Court.
    a. is carved
    b. carved
    c. has been carved
    d. are carved
    e. been carved

179. <u>My family is originally from Nova Scotia.</u>
    a. My family is originally from Nova Scotia.
    b. My family are originally from Nova Scotia.
    c. Originally from Nova Scotia are my family.
    d. Nova Scotia is where my family are from.
    e. My family were originally from Nova Scotia.

180. The Town Council is responsible for <u>traffic control, must evaluate taxes, and generate revenue.</u>
    a. traffic control, must evaluate taxes, and generate revenue.
    b. traffic control, must evaluate taxes, and generate revenue.
    c. must control traffic, evaluate taxes, and generate revenue.
    d. traffic control, evaluating taxes, and generating revenue.
    e. have traffic control, have taxes evaluated, and have generated revenue.

181. Eating carrots <u>gives people good eyesight and to have more energy</u>.
   a. gives people good eyesight and to have more energy.
   b. gives people good eyesight and more energy.
   c. people good eyesight and more energy.
   d. gives good people eyesight and more energy.
   e. gives people good eyesight and has more energy.

182. The snow <u>is falling, and Dave had been sitting</u> by the fire.
   a. is falling, and Dave had been sitting
   b. was falling, and Dave have been sitting
   c. was falling, while Dave sat
   d. is falling, and Dave sat
   e. fell, but Dave had sat

183. <u>To determine the speed of automobiles, radar is often used by the state police.</u>
   a. To determine the speed of automobiles, radar is often used by the state police.
   b. To determine the speed of automobiles, it is often necessary for the state police to use radar.
   c. In determining the speed of automobiles, the use of radar by state police is often employed.
   d. The state police often use radar to determine the speed of automobiles.
   e. Radar by state police in determining the speed of automobiles is often used.

184. Everyone signed the petition before <u>submitting</u> to the city council.
   a. submitting
   b. one submits it
   c. you submit it
   d. we will submit it
   e. we submitted it

185. I have a cross-training exercise program: <u>I swim laps, play tennis, the weight machines, and bicycle riding.</u>
   a. I swim laps, play tennis, the weight machines, and bicycle riding.
   b. I swim laps, play tennis, lift weights, and ride a bicycle.
   c. I swim laps, play tennis, I lift weights, and bicycle riding is a change.
   d. swimming laps, tennis, lifting weights, and the bicycle.
   e. swim laps, play tennis, lifting weights, and riding a bicycle.

186. We all arrived at the theater on time, but before we bought our tickets, Candace <u>says that she's changed her mind and doesn't</u> want to see the movie after all.
   a. says that she's changed her mind and doesn't
   b. said that she had changed her mind and didn't
   c. is saying that she'd changed her mind and doesn't
   d. told us that she is changing her mind and didn't
   e. tells us that she had changed her mind and doesn't

187. State Senator Partridge wished <u>to insure the people that their tax dollars would be spent wisely.</u>
   a. to insure the people that their tax dollars would be spent wisely.
   b. that the people would be insured of tax dollars wisely spent.
   c. in assuring the people, that their tax dollars would be wisely spent.
   d. to assure the people that he would spend their tax dollars wisely.
   e. to assure and promise the people of his intentions to spend their tax dollars wisely.

188. Because he was given a local anesthetic, <u>Josh was conscience throughout the operation.</u>
   a. Josh was conscience throughout the operation.
   b. Josh had a conscience during the operation.
   c. the operation was completed with Josh consciousness.
   d. the operation was done while Josh held consciousness.
   e. Josh remained conscious throughout the operation.

SET 17 (Answers begin on page 170.)
Find the sentence that has a mistake in grammar or usage. Mark choice **d** if you find no mistakes.

189. **a.** No, it's not true.
   b. The curtain closed, and the people will applaud.
   c. My sister is a nurse practitioner.
   d. No mistakes.

190. **a.** They talked through the entire movie.
   b. The plants in this garden does not require much water.
   c. She always brings turkey sandwiches for lunch.
   d. No mistakes.

191. a. What time is it?
   b. The dog lost it's collar.
   c. Shut the door!
   d. No mistakes.

192. a. The cow ate corn.
   b. Joanne loves dessert.
   c. When I get there.
   d. No mistakes.

193. a. The kettle is boiling.
   b. He should of read the directions.
   c. Why is he always so rude?
   d. No mistakes.

194. a. Tomorrow is a Holiday.
   b. Katherine started her new job today.
   c. Politics is boring.
   d. No mistakes.

195. a. David and Mickey danced in the street.
   b. Here is the photographs I wanted to show you.
   c. My grandfather owns a 1967 Mustang.
   d. No mistakes.

196. a. It has not rained since last April.
   b. The jurors walked solemnly into the room.
   c. Had we known, we would not have come.
   d. No mistakes.

197. a. The dog's barking woke us.
   b. Ursula has broke one of your plates.
   c. The sun rose from behind the mountain.
   d. No mistakes.

198. a. After we sat down to eat dinner, the phone rung.
   b. "Keep a positive attitude," he always says.
   c. Sign here.
   d. No mistakes.

199. **a.** The children's books are over there.
      b. She missed the bus and arrives late.
      c. There is hardly enough food for a mouse.
      d. No mistakes.

200. **a.** The winners were announced yesterday.
      b. Liam is the only one of the boys who were chosen.
      c. Although Nick was not selected, he was happy for the others.
      d. No mistakes.

201. **a.** He shook the crumbs from the tablecloth.
      b. We will strive to do our best.
      c. I see that Fred has wore his old shoes.
      d. No mistakes.

202. **a.** When I heard the alarm, I jump out of bed.
      b. Mr. Fox is the president of his own company.
      c. At night, I listened to jazz on the radio.
      d. No mistakes.

SET 18 (Answers begin on page 170.)
Choose the sentence that is the most clearly written and has the best construction.

203. **a.** All the children got out their rugs and took a nap.
      b. All the children have gotten out their rugs and took a nap.
      c. All the children got out their rugs and have taken a nap.
      d. All the children gotten out their rugs and taken a nap.

204. **a.** At first I was liking the sound of the wind, but later it got on my nerves.
      b. At first I liked the sound of the wind, but later it has gotten on my nerves.
      c. At first I like the sound of the wind, but later it got on my nerves.
      d. At first I liked the sound of the wind, but later it got on my nerves.

205. **a.** I became ill from eating too many fried clams.
      b. I became ill from eaten too many fried clams.
      c. I ate too many fried clams and becoming ill.
      d. I ate too many fried clams and become ill.

206. **a.** As the old saying goes, a cat may look at a king.
  b. A cat looking at a king, according to the old saying.
  c. The old saying being, a cat may look at a king.
  d. A cat looking at a king, in the old saying.

207. **a.** A longer happier life, caused by one's owning a pet.
  b. Owning a pet, for one to live a longer, happier life.
  c. To live a longer, happier life by one's owning a pet.
  d. Owning a pet can help one live a longer, happier life.

208. **a.** One of the first modern detectives in literature were created by Edgar Allan Poe.
  b. One of the first modern detectives in literature was created by Edgar Allan Poe.
  c. Edgar Allan Poe having created one of the first modern detectives in literature.
  d. In literature, one of the first modern detectives, created by Edgar Allan Poe.

209. **a.** My brother and I going to see the ball game.
  b. My brother and I are going to see the ball game.
  c. My brother and I seeing the ball game.
  d. My brother and I to the ball game.

210. **a.** I'm not as tall as Ted.
  b. Ted, being taller than me.
  c. I'm as tall, but not like Ted.
  d. Ted is tall, but not me.

211. **a.** Please go to the movies with Mike and me.
  b. Please go to the movies with me and Mike.
  c. Please go to the movies with Mike and I.
  d. Mike and me are going to the movies.

212. **a.** We ate the popcorn and watch the movie.
  b. While watching the movie, the popcorn was eaten.
  c. Popcorn, while watching the movie, was eaten.
  d. We ate the popcorn while we watched the movie.

SET 19 (Answers begin on page 171.)

For the following questions, choose the underlined part of the sentence that contains a grammatical error. Choose choice **e** if there are no errors.

213. All <u>employees</u> with two <u>years'</u> experience <u>are entitled</u> to full <u>benefits</u>,
       a   b   c   d
including health insurance, life insurance, a retirement plan, and stock options. <u>No error.</u>
                                                                                                      e

214. "<u>Their</u> on the <u>way</u>," Tom said. "<u>We'll</u> need to <u>get ready.</u>" <u>No error.</u>
          a   b   c   d   e

215. The perimeter <u>of a square</u> <u>is determined</u> by the <u>lengths</u> of <u>it's</u> sides.
                               a   b   c   d
<u>No error.</u>
    e

216. My brother <u>thinks</u> <u>it's</u> <u>going to</u> snow <u>tomorrow.</u> <u>No error.</u>
                         a   b   c   d   e

217. Last spring, my <u>cousin and I</u> packed <u>the tent, the</u> sleeping <u>bags, and</u>
                               a   b   c
a cooler filled with food and headed <u>west.</u> <u>No error.</u>
                                                          d   e

218. <u>Because</u> of the cost, <u>we</u> decided <u>not</u> to <u>go.</u> <u>No error.</u>
          a   b   c   d   e

219. <u>Each</u> student <u>should turn</u> in <u>their</u> own homework, <u>according</u> to
        a   b   c   d
instructions. <u>No error.</u>
                       e

220. <u>I gave</u> <u>a copy</u> of <u>Tom's</u> novel <u>to</u> my sister. <u>No error.</u>
        a   b   c   d   e

221. The Pilgrims <u>signed</u> the Mayflower Pact <u>to formalize</u> and commit
                          a   b
<u>themselves</u> to <u>there</u> new government <u>No error.</u>
        c   d   e

222. Last summer around the <u>end of July,</u> my <u>brother,</u> my Aunt Clarissa,
                                    a   **b**

and <u>me</u> jumped into the Ford <u>station wagon and</u> headed out of the
     c   **d**

city. <u>No error.</u>
       e

223. The term "blood type" <u>refers to</u> one of the many groups <u>into which</u>
                            a   **b**

a <u>person's</u> blood <u>can be categorized,</u> based on the presence or
       c   **d**

absence of specific antigens. <u>No error.</u>
                             e

224. As you use <u>them,</u> remember that this glossary <u>is intended to be</u> a
                a   **b**

guide and that <u>nothing</u> in it is is <u>absolute.</u> <u>No error.</u>
                 d   **e**

225. The chances of <u>being victimized</u> are slim, but if <u>your</u> not careful,
                 a   **b**

airport thieves—<u>who</u> look like <u>ordinary travelers</u>—can make off with
              c   **d**

your purse, your wallet, your phone card, and all your credit

cards. <u>No error.</u>
         e

226. The distinct geology of Cape Cod <u>began to form</u> about 20,000
                                       a

years ago when the Wisconsin Glacier, up to two miles thick,
pushed <u>its</u> way <u>south</u> from Canada, <u>stopped, and then</u> slowly
      b   **c**   **d**

receded. <u>No error.</u>
          e

227. <u>Although</u> this <u>was</u> an <u>unusually dry</u> summer, the corn crop was not
     a   **b**   **c**

<u>seriously</u> damaged. <u>No error.</u>
  d   **e**

SET 20 (Answers begin on page 172.)
Fill in the blank with the correct pronoun.

228. That fine circus elephant now belongs to my sister and _____.
    a. I
    b. me
    c. mine
    d. myself

229. The person _____ made these delicious candied figs has my vote.
    a. that
    b. whom
    c. who
    d. whose

230. The flowers have all lost _____ petals.
    a. its
    b. their
    c. there
    d. it's

231. George and Michael left _____ backpacks at school.
    a. his
    b. their
    c. there
    d. its

232. How much does _____ hat cost?
    a. which
    b. those
    c. that
    d. them

233. We arranged the flowers and placed _____ in the center of the table.
    a. it
    b. this
    c. them
    d. that

234. _____ met more than ten years ago at a mutual friend's birthday party.
  a. Her and I
  b. Her and me
  c. She and me
  d. She and I

235. My parents approved of _____ taking guitar lessons.
  a. my
  b. me
  c. I
  d. mine

SET 21 (Answers begin on page 172.)
Replace the underlined words with the phrase that best completes the sentence. Choose choice **a** if the sentence is correct as is.

236. It was either Kendra or Zoë who <u>brought their </u>volleyball to the picnic.
  a. brought their
  b. brought her
  c. brought their
  d. brang their
  e. brang her

237. <u>Whose car will you take when you drive to their</u> house?
  a. Whose car will you take when you drive to their
  b. Whose car will you take when you drive to there
  c. Who's car will you take when you drive to their
  d. Who's car will take when you drive to there
  e. Which car will you take when you drive to there

238. A person who studies hard <u>will reach their goals</u>.
  a. will reach their goals
  b. will reach their goal
  c. will reach his or her goals
  d. reached their goal
  e. had reached their goal

CONJUNCTIONS

Conjunctions connect two clauses in a sentence. Some common conjunctions:

and	if	while
but	although	since

239. Two angles with the same degree measurement is said to be congruent.
    a. Two angles with the same degree measurement is said to be congruent.
    b. With two angles of the same degree measurement, they are said to be congruent.
    c. When two angles have the same degree measurement, they are said to be congruent.
    d. They are congruent when the two angles are said to have the same degree measurement.
    e. Two angles with the same degree measurement are said to be congruent.

240. The friendship between Andre and Robert began when he and his family moved to Ohio.
    a. The friendship between Andre and Robert began when he and his
    b. Andre and Robert's friendship began when he and his
    c. The friendship among the two boys began when he and his
    d. The friendship between Andre and Robert began when Robert and his
    e. Andre and Robert's friendship began when their

SET 22 (Answers begin on page 173.)

Find the sentence that has a mistake in grammar or usage. Mark choice **d** if you find no mistakes.

241. **a.** The weather forecast looks good for Tuesday.
     b. Her hair is a terrible mess!
     c. My mother will take Dan and I to school tomorrow.
     d. No mistakes.

242. **a.** My favorite subject is English.
     b. The band is playing its best today.
     c. I saw Fred's sister at the mall.
     d. No mistakes.

243. **a.** They're not going to join us.
     b. Don't eat too much jam!
     c. Wear the plaid shirt with that tie.
     d. No mistakes.

244. **a.** Their ship came in.
     b. Which glass is yours?
     c. "Betty and me will be there tomorrow," she said.
     d. No mistakes.

245. **a.** Sheila's sister wanted to accompany us to the party.
     b. Who's scarf is this?
     c. "Be sure to wear something comfortable," she said.
     d. No mistakes.

246. **a.** The main problem Jim had was too many parking tickets.
     b. As the bears ran toward us, it was growling.
     c. Try using less butter next time.
     d. No mistakes.

247. **a.** Kamala was the most intelligent person in the group.
     b. The Eiffel Tower is in Paris, France.
     c. Nick Carraway is a character in *The Great Gatsby*.
     d. No mistakes.

248. **a.** They weren't the only ones who didn't like the movie.
  b. "Please come back another time," Aunt Julie begged.
  c. "Threes a crowd," he always says.
  d. No mistakes.

249. **a.** The first house on the street is there's.
  b. I love the fireworks on the Fourth of July.
  c. My grandparents live in San Juan, Puerto Rico.
  d. No mistakes.

250. **a.** Either Cassie nor I heard the door open.
  b. How many people signed the Declaration of Independence?
  c. Draw up a plan before you make your decision.
  d. No mistakes.

251. **a.** It's not my fault that you and him got caught.
  b. "Do you brush twice a day?" Dr. Evans asked.
  c. What's the weather report?
  d. No mistakes.

252. **a.** Couldn't you arrive fashionably late?
  b. You're assumption is correct.
  c. I know that Bowser will be well treated.
  d. No mistakes.

253. **a.** We invited Mayor Chen to speak at our school.
  b. The alarm sounded, and the firefighters jumped into the truck.
  c. The committee members should work as hard as one can.
  d. No mistakes.

254. **a.** He wore two different shoes to class.
  b. Rhonda's sister bought a new Pontiac.
  c. Lake Superior is the largest of the Great Lakes.
  d. No mistakes.

255. **a.** She and I have been friends for more than ten years.
  b. Is that one of the O'Farrell children?
  c. They took too much time to answer.
  d. No mistakes.

SET 23 (Answers begin on page 173.)

Choose the sentence that is the most clearly written and has the best construction.

256. **a.** Although I'm old enough, I don't drink.
    b. I don't drink, even though I'm old enough.
    c. I'm old enough, although I don't drink.
    d. Being old enough, I don't drink.

257. **a.** When it won't rain, the sky was full of clouds.
    b. Since the sky was full of clouds, it wouldn't rain.
    c. It won't rain because the sky is full of clouds.
    d. The sky is full of clouds, yet it won't rain.

258. **a.** In search of the missing teenagers, who still had not been found through snake-ridden underbrush all day, the exhausted volunteers had struggled.
    b. All day the exhausted volunteers had struggled through snake-ridden underbrush in search of the missing teenagers, who still had not been found.
    c. All day the exhausted volunteers had struggled through snake-ridden underbrush who still had not been found in searching for the missing teenagers.
    d. The exhausted volunteers who still had not found in search of the missing teenagers when they had struggled through snake-ridden underbrush.

259. **a.** One New York publisher have estimated that 50,000 to 60,000 people in the United States want an anthology that includes the complete works of William Shakespeare.
    b. One New York publisher has estimated that 50,000 to 60,000 people in the United States want a anthology that includes the complete works of William Shakespeare.
    c. One New York publisher has estimated that 50,000 to 60,000 people in the United States want an anthology that includes the complete works of William Shakespeare.
    d. One New York publisher has estimated that 50,000 to 60,000 people in the United States want an anthology that included the complete works of William Shakespeare.

4

Modifiers

Adjectives and adverbs modify subjects or their actions in a sentence. In the sentence, "The orange and striped cat leapt nimbly across the dresser," adjectives and adverbs specify what kind of cat (an "orange and striped cat") and how that cat leapt ("nimbly"). All too often, adjectives and adverbs are confused for one another. However, in this section, you will put each in its proper place and in its proper form.

First, you have to know the definition of a modifier:

✓ A **modifier** describes or limits another word.→*Lily* is a subject. Add the word *tiger* before lily and the subject is modified: It is now a specific type of lily. *Pushed* is an action word. Add *gently* and the action is limited: It is now a softer action. Put the subject, its action, and the modifiers all together and the sentence reads: *Unlike its fierce namesake, the tiger lily pushed its head gently through the soil.*

Types of Modifiers

✓ **Adjectives** modify nouns or pronouns. (*Hint:* An *adjective* answers one of three questions: which one, what kind, or how many?)

✓ **Adverbs** modify verbs, adjectives, other adverbs, or whole groups of words. (*Hint:* An adverb answers one of four questions: where, when, how, or to what extent?)

✓ **Comparatives** are adjectives and adverbs used to compare two things.→*He's the* better *of the two.*

✓ **Superlatives** are adjectives and adverbs used to compare more than two things.→*He's the* best *of the three.*

BEGINNING SENTENCES WITH DEPENDENT CLAUSES

Do not, as a general rule, place a dependent clause at the beginning of a sentence. Words that should not begin a sentence include:

because	while	wherea.	unless
although	when	after	since

Follow these guidelines and you will do well (*well* describes the verb *to do*; therefore, it is an adverb!):

✓ Always identify whether a modifier describes or limits a sentence's subject or its action.

✓ Use *good* and *bad* to describe nouns.

✓ Use *well* and *badly* to describe verbs, except when *well* means "fit" or "healthy." When *well* describes a state of being, it is an adjective.→*With repetition, you will soon write well. Well* describes how the subject writes; it is an adverb. *After two months of physical therapy, Bob was well. Well* describes Bob's state of being; it is an adjective.

✓ Use an adjective after a *linking verb*. The following words are linking verbs when they express a state of being: *look, sound, smell, feel, taste, appear, seem, become, grow, turn, prove, remain,* and *stay.*→*Howard leaned over and surreptitiously smelled Lee; she smelled sweet. Surreptitiously* describes how Howard sniffed at the other person; in this case, it is an adverb because it describes the act of smelling. *Sweet* describes Lee; the word *smell* links the adjective back to the subject.

✓ Use the adjective *fewer* to describe plural nouns and the adjective *less* to describe singular nouns.

✓ Use the word *number* to describe plural nouns and the word *amount* to describe singular nouns.

✓ Add *-er* to a modifier or place the word *more* or *less* before the modifier to compare two things. This creates a comparison. (*Hint*: One to two syllable modifiers usually receive the suffix *-er*; modifiers with more than two syllables use *more* or *less* before them.)

✓ Add *-est* to a modifier or place the word *most* or *least* before the modifier to indicate the extreme degree of a thing (*Hint*: One to two syllable modifiers receive *-est*; modifiers with more than two syllables use *most* or *least* before them.)

✓ Avoid double comparatives or double superlatives. Adding the suffix *-er* or *-est* to a modifier and preceding the modifier with *more* or *most* is redundant.→*Lindsey amazed the class with her grammatical skills; she was the most smartest person they had ever seen.* Lindsey is already *the smartest*. *Most* also means smartest—the phrase *most smartest* is redundant.

✓ Avoid double negatives unless you mean to express the positive.→*Tom hardly did not feel tense whenever he approached grammar. Hardly* and *did not* cancel each other out. The sentence really reads: *Tom felt tense whenever approaching grammar.*

✓ Avoid illogical comparisons. Some words already indicate an extreme degree; like double comparatives and double superlatives, adding the word *more* or *most* before such words is redundant.→*Some women believe Brad Pitt is more perfect than Matt Damon.* There are not degrees of perfection; one is either perfect or not perfect. However, one can more nearly approach perfection than someone else.

SET 24 (Answers begin on page 174.)

For the following questions, choose the underlined part of the sentence that contains a grammatical error. Choose choice **e** if there are no errors.

260. <u>Frightened,</u> the little boy screamed <u>loud</u> as his <u>neighbor's</u> friendly
       a   b   c

<u>eighty-pound dog</u> bounded up the sidewalk. <u>No error.</u>
      d   e

261. Gwen's friend Luke—<u>once the star</u> quarterback of his college football
                         a

team and now a <u>successful restaurateur</u>—<u>owns</u> ten restaurants and
                    b   c

<u>has published</u> three award-winning cookbooks. <u>No error.</u>
      d   e

262. <u>Three girls</u> recently joined the basketball team, <u>but</u> Frieda <u>is still</u>
      a   b   c
the <u>taller.</u> <u>No error.</u>
   d   e

263. <u>The top of</u> the mountain <u>was</u> shrouded in fog, <u>so</u> we <u>could not</u> see
    a   b   c   d
the flag. <u>No error.</u>
       e

264. <u>Bill is</u> the <u>smarter</u> of the two, but <u>Mike is</u> <u>still</u> very bright. <u>No error.</u>
   a   b   c   d   e

265. The love seat is now <u>being installed</u> in some New York movie theaters,
                     a
<u>giving</u> couples the option of lifting the arm <u>between</u> the seats to
 b   c
create a <u>more cozier</u> viewing experience. <u>No error.</u>
     d   e

266. Some buildings, <u>such as</u> the White House, Saint Paul's <u>Cathedral,</u>
              a   b
and the Taj Mahal, deserve to be preserved not only because of <u>their</u>
                                          c
artistic excellence <u>but also</u> because of their symbolic associations.
                d
<u>No error.</u>
  e

267. "I don't feel <u>good</u>," <u>the boy</u> <u>said</u> <u>quietly.</u> <u>No error.</u>
            a   b   c   d   e

268. In this cookbook, <u>you'll discover</u> colorful, easy to <u>prepare, and</u> great-
                a   b
tasting recipes <u>for even</u> your <u>more</u> diet-conscious guests. <u>No error.</u>
        c   d   e

269. <u>When</u> the professor called out his name, <u>he walked</u> rather <u>hesitant</u>
   a   b   c
to the front of the room and stood <u>there</u> shaking. <u>No error.</u>
                      d   e

270. The puppy had been treated <u>bad</u> by <u>its</u> previous <u>owner, but</u> the
                                    a   **b**   **c**

people at the animal shelter <u>worked hard</u> to find a loving home for
                                       d

little Scotty. <u>No error.</u>
                 e

SET 25 (Answers begin on page 174.)
Fill in the blank with the correct adjective or adverb.

271. In many popular movies today, the heroes are _____ armed
than the villains.
   a. more heavily
   b. more heavy
   c. heavier
   d. more heavier

272. The cake that I made last week tasted _____ than the one I
made today.
   a. best
   b. more better
   c. better
   d. more good

273. After winning the yo-yo contest, Lydia skipped _____ down the
street.
   a. happy
   b. happiest
   c. more happily
   d. happily

274. Of the three brothers, Andre is the _____.
   a. taller
   b. tallest
   c. more tall
   d. most tallest

275. Riding the Tornado at the amusement park was _____ than I thought it would be.
  a. more terrifying
  b. more terrifyingly
  c. terrifying
  d. most terrifying

276. This year our company sold _____ magazine subscriptions than ever before.
  a. less
  b. lesser
  c. few
  d. fewer

SET 26 (Answers begin on page 175.)
Replace the underlined words with the word or phrase that is grammatically correct. Choose choice **a** if the sentence is correct as is.

277. The book had <u>a frighteningly and unhappy ending</u>.
  a. a frighteningly and unhappy ending.
  b. a frighteningly and unhappily ending.
  c. an ending that was frightening and unhappily.
  d. a frightening and unhappy ending.
  e. an ending that was frightening and it was also an unhappy one.

278. Since her graduation from business school last spring, Adela has become known <u>as the more important</u> member of her graduating class.
  a. as the more important
  b. as the most important
  c. as the most importantly
  d. as the more importantly
  e. like the most important

279. Surprisingly, my younger sister dresses <u>more conservatively than I do.</u>
  a. more conservatively than I do.
  b. more conservative than I do.
  c. more conservative than me.
  d. more conservatively than me.
  e. the most conservative in opposition to me.

280. <u>There wasn't nothing that could have been easier.</u>
   a. There wasn't nothing that could have been easier.
   b. There was nothing that could have been more easier.
   c. Nothing could have been more easier.
   d. Nothing couldn't have been more easy.
   e. Nothing could have been easier.

281. <u>I was clearly the happiest person in the crowd.</u>
   a. I was clearly the happiest person in the crowd.
   b. It was clear that I was the happier person in the crowd.
   c. Of all the people in the crowd, I was clearly the happier.
   d. In the crowd, clearly, I was the happier person.
   e. Of all the people in the crowd, clearly, I being the happiest.

282. Our team scored <u>less baskets today than we did</u> last Tuesday.
   a. less baskets today than we did
   b. today less baskets than were scored
   c. fewer baskets today then on
   d. fewer baskets today than we did
   e. a lesser number of baskets today then we did

283. Strip mining, the <u>cheaper</u> method of mining, is controversial because it jeopardizes the environment.
   a. cheaper
   b. more cheap
   c. most cheapest
   d. cheapest
   e. more cheaply

SET 27 (Answers begin on page 176.)
Find the sentence that has a mistake in grammar or usage. Mark choice **d** if
you find no mistakes.

284. **a.** The steam rose up from the hot pavement.
   b. She put the kitten down carefully beside its mom.
   c. Neither of us is going to the party.
   d. No mistakes.

285.   **a.** The lost dog wandered sad through the streets.
      b. Frustrated, Boris threw his pencil across the room.
      c. We'll stop at their house first.
      d. No mistakes.

286.   **a.** I don't want to participate no longer.
      b. If you're not sure, look in the dictionary.
      c. "I will try to do better," Lauren promised.
      d. No mistakes.

287.   **a.** The boy wasn't feeling well.
      b. I am the best player on the team.
      c. That is the brightest tie I've ever seen!
      d. No mistakes.

288.   **a.** This is the stronger of the two.
      b. Pearl ran as quickly as possible.
      c. There are more people here today than there were yesterday.
      d. No mistakes.

289.   **a.** This paper has less mistakes than your last one.
      b. His efforts were frenzied.
      c. That is the most audacious comment I've heard yet.
      d. No mistakes.

290.   **a.** One car is quicker than the other.
      b. I'm feeling sleepy.
      c. Don't chew so loudly!
      d. No mistakes.

ADJECTIVES

Words that modify nouns, adding information. Some examples:

a *pretty* picture   a *religious* holiday

a *hot* da.   a *funny* song

291. **a.** Between the three of us, we should find the answer.
 b. Alberto laughed loudly when he saw us.
 c. They're looking for another apartment.
 d. No mistakes.

292. **a.** The Adirondacks are mountains in New York.
 b. President Carter gave the Panama Canal back to Panama.
 c. That river is terribly polluted.
 d. No mistakes.

293. **a.** *Trading Spaces* is probably the most daring show on television.
 b. Which color do you like better, the teal or the flamingo pink?
 c. Mango-peach berry juice is the most awfulest drink.
 d. No mistakes.

ADVERBS

Words that modify verbs, adding information. Some examples:

drive *fast*	sleep *well*
jump *high*	play *hard*

Paragraph Development

Paragraphs are groups of related sentences that form complete units. They usually support the main ideas of an essay, article, or story; however, every paragraph has an identity and an idea of its own. A paragraph is like a miniature essay. For practice in paragraph development and unity, Section 5 will ask you to identify the best topic sentence for a particular paragraph, find the sentence that best develops a topic, and eliminate the sentence that does not belong. You will also choose the best order for a group of sentences. The guideline below will help you to organize your paragraphs. Paragraphs and essays are similar in structure, so these guidelines can be applied to the organization of an entire essay.

✓ Write a paragraph to explore a single idea using a **topic sentence** near the beginning of the paragraph.

✓ Maintain **paragraph unity**, the logical development of a single idea in a group of related sentences, by using:

- a **consistent organizing strategy**. Paragraphs present ideas and group detailed information necessary to develop ideas. Organizing strategies arrange that information into logical and easy-to-anticipate patterns. These patterns can be top to bottom, left to right, near to far, then to now, beginning to ending, general to specific, least important to most important, least familiar to most familiar, or simplest to most complex. Other strategies use stories, descriptions, examples, definitions, categorizations, comparisons and contrasts, or causes and effects to logically organize information. As you become more proficient at writing, you will probably incorporate more than one strategy in a paragraph.

- **parallelisms.** By arranging sentences in identical patterns, a writer can convey that two different things are equally important. Patterning sentence structure is called parallelism.→*Bob quickly ran to the store; Alex also quickly ran to the store. It was a race to see who was faster.*

- **repeated words or word groups.** Repeating words is a tactic similar to parallelism, except that repetition can occur anywhere in a sentence.→*Mark persevered in practice. The work was hard—but he persevered. The pain grew intense, but still, he persevered.*

- **transitional phrases or words** to connect sentences and ideas→ *First, Katie gathered the ingredients. Then she assembled the meal.*

✓ **Important:** Try not to shift a pronoun's case or a verb's tense in a paragraph unless your organizing strategy requires it.

SET 28 (Answers begin on page 176.)

For each of the following paragraphs, choose the topic sentence that best fits the rest of the paragraph.

_____. Residents have been directed to use the new plastic bins as their primary recycling containers. These new containers will make picking up recyclables faster and easier.

294. **a.** The city has distributed standardized recycling containers to all households.

b. Recycling has become a way of life for most people.

c. While most Americans recycle, they also use more resources than residents of other countries.

d. Even small cities have begun recycling to pick up used glass, plastic, and paper.

_____. Telecommuters produce, on average, 20% more than if they were to work in an office. Their flexible schedule allows them to balance both their family and work responsibilities.

295. **a.** People who work in offices make up a large part of the U.S. workforce.
b. Office workers who telecommute from their own homes are more productive and have greater flexibility.
c. Many companies now offer their employees benefits that were not available just a few years ago.
d. One of the biggest problems in corporate America is the lack of skilled office workers.

_____. No search of a person's home or personal effects may be conducted without a written search warrant. This means that a judge must justify a search before it can be conducted.

296. **a.** There is an old saying that a person's home is his or her castle.
b. Much of the U.S. legal system was based on the old British system.
c. The Fourth Amendment to the Constitution protects citizens against unreasonable searches.
d. "Personal effects" is a term that refers to the belongings of a person.

_____. You must imitate as closely as possible the parents' methods of feeding. First, hold the beak open using thumb and forefinger. Then, introduce food into the beak with tweezers or an eyedropper.

297. **a.** Recently, I read an article about baby birds.
b. Hand-rearing wounded or orphaned baby birds requires skill.
c. Baby birds are very special creatures, and they are also very small.
d. I have been told that you should not touch a baby bird that has fallen out of its nest.

_____. All waves, though, have common characteristics that govern their height. The height of a wave is determined by its speed, the distance it travels, and the length of time the wind blows.

298. **a.** Currents, unlike waves, are caused by steady winds or temperature fluctuations.
 b. Tsunamis used to be called tidal waves.
 c. Ocean waves can vary from tiny ripples to powerful, raging swells.
 d. A breaker is when a wave gets top-heavy and tips over.

_____. When people respect the law too much, they will follow it blindly. They will say that the majority has decided on this law and therefore I must obey it. They will not stop to consider whether or not the law is fair.

299. **a.** Some people say there is too little respect for the law, but I say there is too much respect for it.
 b. Sometimes, a judge will decide that a law is unfair.
 c. I believe that the majority of the people in this country do not understand what it means to have respect for other people.
 d. Most of the laws passed at the end of the twentieth century are fair laws.

Gary was a very distinguished looking man with a touch of gray at the temples. Even in his early fifties, he was still the one to turn heads. He enjoyed spending most of his time admiring his profile in the mirror. In fact, he considered his good looks to be his second most important asset in the world. The first, however, was money. He was lucky in this area, too, having been born into a wealthy family. _____. He loved the power his wealth had given him. He could buy whatever he desired, be that people, places, or things. Gary checked that mirror often and felt great delight with what he saw.

300. **a.** Gary's gray hair was his worst characteristic.
 b. Conceit was the beginning and the end of Gary's character— conceit of person and situation.
 c. Gary felt blessed to be wealthy and the joy consumed his every thought.
 d. The only objects of Gary's respect were others who held positions in society.

The term *spices* is a pleasant one, whether it connotes fine French cuisine or a down-home, cinnamon-flavored apple pie. _____. Individuals have traveled the world seeking exotic spices for profit and, in searching, have changed the course of history. Indeed, to gain control of lands harboring new spices, nations have actually gone to war.

301. **a.** The taste and aroma of spices are the main elements that make food such a source of fascination and pleasure.
  b. The term might equally bring to mind Indian curry made thousands of miles away and those delicious barbecued ribs sold around the corner.
  c. It is exciting to find a good cookbook and experiment with spices from other lands—indeed, it is one way to travel around the globe!
  d. The history of spices, however, is another matter altogether, often exciting and filled with danger and intrigue.

_____. The best way to begin is by selecting a working space with good lighting. Proper tools are also important, and you will want to purchase some quality paint brushes and a selection of quality paints.

302. **a.** Painting models and miniatures is a satisfying hobby.
  b. Low quality painting tools can be frustrating.
  c. Good lighting is important when painting.
  d. Don't buy paintbrushes on sale.

_____. The farm dates back to the Revolutionary War, when it was owned by Silas Wheeler. Wheeler himself fought in several early battles of the war, but his farm is best remembered as the site of an important battle, when the Colonial forces won a decisive victory against the British.

303. **a.** Farms are places where we can learn many things.
  b. Wheeler Farm is an important historical landmark.
  c. Silas Wheeler was an American patriot.
  d. The Revolutionary War made many people famous.

_____. They are certainly useful for keeping the grass short, yet the spinning blade of any power mower can sever fingers, toes, and even a hand. Proper safety measures must be followed at all times when using a power lawn mower.

304. a. Wear safety shoes when cutting the lawn.
   b. Power lawn mowers are useful tools, but they can also be very dangerous.
   c. The history of lawn mowers is very interesting.
   d. Short grass is important for the environment.

_____. Effective immediately, all vacation time must be pre-approved by an employee's immediate supervisor. No vacations will be approved unless the employee has completed his or her probationary period, and employees can no longer borrow against future vacation days.

305. a. The company's vacation policy has been changed.
   b. Employees on probation must not take vacations.
   c. Borrowing from future vacations is not allowed.
   d. We used to do things differently, but now we don't.

_____. Hearsay that depends on the statement's truthfulness is inadmissible because the witness does not appear in court and swear an oath to tell the truth. This means that his or her demeanor when making the statement is not visible to the jury, the accuracy of the statement cannot be tested under cross-examination, and to introduce it would be to deprive the accused of the constitutional right to confront the accuser.

306. a. Hearsay evidence is not acceptable in a criminal trial because the witness cannot be cross-examined.
   b. Hearsay evidence in a trial is inadmissible because there is too great a chance that it will be false.
   c. The definition of hearsay evidence is the "secondhand reporting of a statement" and is sometimes allowable.
   d. Hearsay evidence, which is the secondhand reporting of a statement, is allowed in court only when the truth of the statement is irrelevant.

_____. Any truck that finishes its assigned route before the end of the workers' shift will return to the sanitation lot, where supervisors will provide materials for workers to use in cleaning off the graffiti. Because the length of time it takes to complete different routes varies, trucks will no longer be assigned to a specific route but will be rotated among the routes. Therefore, workers should no longer leave personal items in the trucks, as they will not necessarily be using the same truck each day as they did in the past.

307. **a.** Graffiti on city trucks is unsightly and gives city residents a poor impression of the Sanitation Department.
   b. The Sanitation Department greatly appreciates city workers' extra efforts in cleaning graffiti off the city trucks.
   c. Beginning next month, the Sanitation Department will institute a program intended to remove the graffiti from sanitation trucks.
   d. City workers should keep a sharp lookout for persons spray-painting graffiti on Sanitation Department trucks.

_____. One type of tickler system is the index-card file with 12 large dividers, one for each month, and 31 small dividers, one for each day. Whenever secretaries need to schedule a reminder, they jot it down on a card and place it behind the appropriate divider. Each morning, they review the reminders for that particular day.

308. **a.** As busy secretaries, we cannot expect to remember all the details of our daily responsibilities without some help.
   b. At the beginning of the day, good secretaries review and organize the tasks they must attend to during that day.
   c. The word _tickler_ perfectly describes the organizational system to which it refers.
   d. All secretaries need a good reminder system, sometimes known as a tickler system because it tickles the memory.

_____. Space shuttle astronauts, because they spend only about a week in space, undergo minimal wasting of bone and muscle. But when longer stays in microgravity or zero gravity are contemplated, as in the proposed space station or a two-year roundtrip voyage to Mars, these problems are of particular concern because they could become acute. Fortunately, studies show that muscle atrophy can be kept largely at bay with appropriate exercise. Unfortunately, bone loss caused by reduced gravity cannot.

309. a. Space flight, especially if it is prolonged, can be hazardous to the health of the astronauts.
b. The tissues of human beings are ill-prepared for the stresses placed upon them by space flight.
c. In space flight, astronauts must deal with two vexing physiological foes—muscle atrophy and bone loss.
d. Travel on the space shuttle does less damage to an astronaut's bones and muscles than an extended stay on a space station.

_____. Rather, asthma is now understood to be a chronic inflammatory disorder of the airways—that is, inflammation makes the airways chronically sensitive. When these hyper-responsive airways are irritated, air flow is limited, and attacks of coughing, wheezing, chest tightness, and difficulty breathing occur.

310. a. No longer is asthma considered a condition with isolated, acute episodes of bronchospasm.
b. The true nature of asthma has only recently been understood.
c. The true character of asthma is now understood, so there is more hope for a cure than there was in earlier times.
d. No age is exempt from asthma, although it occurs most often in childhood and early adulthood.

_____. Many experts, including those in the American Diabetes Association, recommend that 50 to 60% of daily calories of patients suffering from non-insulin-dependent diabetes come from carbohydrates, 12 to 20% from protein, and no more than 30% from fat. Foods that are rich in carbohydrates, like breads, cereals, fruits, and vegetables, break down into glucose during digestion, causing blood glucose to rise. Additionally, studies have shown that cooked foods raise blood glucose higher than raw, unpeeled foods.

311. a. In 1986, a National Institute of Health panel gave broad recommendations as to the type of diet that is best for non-insulin-dependent diabetics.

　　b. It is extremely important for certain medical patients to watch what they eat.

　　c. A good cookbook is the best friend a non-insulin-dependent diabetes patient can have!

　　d. Non-insulin-dependent diabetes patients can lead long, healthy lives if only they pay attention to their diets.

SET 29 (Answers begin on page 178.)
Choose the answer that best develops the topic sentence given.

312. Indoor pollution sources that release gases or particles into the air are the primary cause of indoor air-quality problems in homes.

　　a. Inadequate ventilation can increase indoor pollutant levels by not bringing in enough outdoor air to dilute emissions from indoor sources.

　　b. Some physicians believe that the dangers of "environmental allergens" are greatly exaggerated.

　　c. Although there are more potential pollution sources today than ever before, environmental activists are working hard to make our world a safer place.

　　d. I'll choose a good, old-fashioned log cabin any day to the kind of squeaky-clean, hermetically-sealed modern condos you find in the big American cities.

313. In the Middle Ages, red hair was associated with evil, so to have red hair was to be in constant danger.

　　a. People with red hair are sometimes singled out and called unflattering nicknames.

　　b. The Middle Ages was a time of great turmoil and people were often summarily executed by being burned at the stake.

　　c. During that time period, people with red hair were sometimes killed because they were thought to be witches.

　　d. Red hair is passed on genetically from parent to child.

314. Many weed killers operate by killing the plant's root, thereby preventing the weed from spreading.

   a. The weed killer is absorbed by the leaves, then travels to the roots.

   b. Proper care must be taken when handling weed killers.

   c. Some weeds don't need water to survive.

   d. Weeds are plants that nobody wants.

315. One of the most fascinating discoveries in modern physics is the idea that light can behave both as particles and as waves.

   a. In order to understand quantum physics, one must know a great deal about mathematics.

   b. What is called "empty space" by laypersons is really not empty at all, but a sea of negative energy electrons.

   c. This idea, first suggested by the French noblemen Louis de Broglie, is counterintuitive, but can be empirically proven.

   d. Some physicists say that nothing is real unless it is observed.

316. The Internet has revolutionized mass communication.

   a. The Internet was not invented by a politician.

   b. E-mail, blogs, chat rooms, and many other tools make it easy to communicate with people.

   c. Communication is a difficult art to learn.

   d. The world's largest computer fills an entire building.

317. There are many good reasons to eat organic food. It tastes great. It is grown and handled according to strict guidelines to ensure that it is safe and pesticide-free. And organic farming respects the balance demanded of a healthy ecosystem.

   a. Many restaurants and supermarkets now carry organic products.

   b. Health-food stores are popping up all over the country.

   c. An organic lifestyle is good for you, and for our world.

   d. Ten years ago, it was much more difficult to find organic food in traditional supermarkets.

318. It is a myth that financial aid for higher education just means getting a loan and going into heavy debt.

   a. It's important for young people to avoid starting out their working lives under a load of indebtedness.

   b. Financial aid is meant to help those students who could otherwise not attend college.

   c. The truth is that students in medicine and law are often able to pay back their student loans in short order.

   d. The fact is that most schools have their own grants and scholarships, which the student doesn't have to pay back, and a large percentage of students get these.

319. This contract will confirm our agreement in connection with your services as freelance writer for the work entitled *Why Kangaroos Can't Fly*.

   a. The title, although rather silly, accurately sums up the tone and style of the book.

   b. You agree to assist us in preparation of the book by developing content for it, based on your zoo-keeping experience.

   c. It is important to have a legal contract before turning your written work over to a publishing company.

   d. This book will make an important contribution to kangaroo lore around the world.

320. America's fascination with reality television is a topic of much discussion. Many think that people tune in simply to keep up-to-date with the latest popular culture trends.

   a. Whether you love it or hate it, reality television is definitely here to stay.

   b. Every season brings several new reality television shows. However, not every one of them succeeds.

   c. Reality television has no redeeming qualities whatsoever. Critics find it shallow, sensationalistic, and mindless.

   d. Ordinary people might also see themselves in these reality television personalities, leading to a sense of exhilaration as they watch their television counterparts achieve celebrity status and win big prizes.

321. Pasta is both delicious and healthy, and it has the added benefit of being easy to prepare.

    a. Pasta was invented in the Middle Ages in Italy.

    b. Tomato sauce is the best topping for spaghetti.

    c. Marathon runners eat pasta before a race.

    d. Most pasta dishes can be prepared in less than 15 minutes.

322. During colonial times in America, juries were encouraged to ask questions of the parties in the courtroom.

    a. The jurors were, in fact, expected to investigate the facts of the case themselves. If jurors conducted an investigation today, we would throw out the case.

    b. Many states are experimenting with new ways to get more people to serve on juries. All eligible voters can be called to serve.

    c. There are usually two attorneys: a prosecutor and a defense attorney. This sometimes makes the courtroom lively.

    d. There were thirteen colonies. Each colony at first had its own legal system.

323. Landscapers do not recommend rose bushes for homeowners who have shade-filled gardens and who don't spend a great deal of time maintaining outdoor plants.

    a. Bugs called *aphids* can destroy roses. However, you can get rid of them by spraying with a solution of water and dish soap.

    b. Gardening can be quite time-consuming. Most gardeners spend hours in their gardens each week.

    c. When these conditions are present, a better choice would be hostas. They are extremely hardy and easy-to-grow shade plants with attractive foliage.

    d. Landscapers can be hired on a weekly or monthly basis to care for lawns and gardens. They can also be hired for a one-time consultation or for a specific lawn or garden project.

324. Ginkgo biloba extract is the most commonly prescribed plant remedy in the world.

    a. There are many plant remedies, including the ones that can be purchased in health-food stores. Not all plant remedies have been approved.

    b. It is a highly refined compound produced from the leaves of the ginkgo tree. Many people take ginkgo to treat conditions such as headaches, asthma, and hearing loss.

    c. Ginkgo has also been widely prescribed in Europe. It has been approved by the German government for the treatment of memory loss.

    d. A 1977 study with ginkgo was conducted with twenty patients. These patients ranged in age from 62 to 85.

325. Cats have the highest level of hygiene of any common domestic pet.

    a. They wash themselves frequently, and never need baths.

    b. The first recorded domesticated cat was in ancient Egypt.

    c. Cats come in many breeds and types.

    d. Most pet stores offer a variety of foods for cats.

SET 30 (Answers begin on page 179.)

For each of the following paragraphs, choose the sentence that does NOT belong.

(1) The cassowary, a solitary, meat-eating creature who makes its home deep in the jungles of New Guinea, hardly seems like a bird at all. **(2)** It is enormous, weighing up to 190 pounds. **(3)** Its plumage is more like hair than feathers; its song is a deep, menacing rumble; and it has lost the capability of flight. **(4)** Human beings have long been fascinated by birds, particularly by their ability to fly.

326.   **a.** Sentence 1

      b. Sentence 2

      c. Sentence 3

      d. Sentence 4

(1) Storytelling should speak first to the heart and only second to the intellect. (2) It should, in Isaac Bashevis Singer's words, "be both clear and profound," and it should also entertain. (3) Many fine writing programs have sprung up across the United States. (4) The new writer should avoid creating pieces that are deliberately obscure and impossible to understand except by a small, elite group of other writers.

327. a. Sentence 1
 b. Sentence 2
 c. Sentence 3
 d. Sentence 4

(1) Caribbean cuisine is a fusion of Spanish, French, African, Amerindian, and Indian cuisine. (2) Many people travel to the Caribbean to enjoy the beautiful beaches and warm weather. (3) A typical dish and one increasingly common outside of the area is "jerk" seasoned meats, commonly chicken. (4) Other popular dishes include curried goat and a soup-like dish called callaloo.

328. a. Sentence 1
 b. Sentence 2
 c. Sentence 3
 d. Sentence 4

(1) Ratatouille is a dish that has grown in popularity over the last few years. (2) It features eggplant, zucchini, tomato, peppers, and garlic, chopped, mixed together, and cooked slowly over low heat. (3) Zucchini is a summer squash and has a smooth, dark green skin. (4) As the vegetables cook slowly, they make their own broth, which may be extended with a little tomato paste.

329. a. Sentence 1
 b. Sentence 2
 c. Sentence 3
 d. Sentence 4

(1) An odd behavior associated with sleep and dreaming is somnambulism, commonly known as sleepwalking. (2) Sleepwalkers suffer from a malfunction in a brain mechanism that monitors the transition from REM to non-REM sleep. (3) REM sleep is vitally important to psychological well-being. (4) Sleepwalking episodes diminish with age and usually cause no serious harm—the worst thing that could happen would be a fall down the stairs.

330.   a. Sentence 1
       b. Sentence 2
       c. Sentence 3
       d. Sentence 4

(1) Lyme disease is sometimes called the *great imitator* because its many symptoms mimic those of other illnesses. (2) When treated, this disease usually presents few or no lingering effects. (3) Left untreated, it can be extremely debilitating and sometimes fatal. (4) One should be very careful when returning from a trek in the woods to check for deer ticks.

331.   a. Sentence 1
       b. Sentence 2
       c. Sentence 3
       d. Sentence 4

(1) The harp is a musical instrument that has an upright triangular frame. (2) Its strings are positioned perpendicular to the sounding board. (3) Harps are found in Africa, Europe, North and South America, and a few parts of Asia. (4) Its beautiful sound, which is capable of stirring great emotion, might bring tears to your eyes.

332.   a. Sentence 1
       b. Sentence 2
       c. Sentence 3
       d. Sentence 4

(1) In the summer, the northern hemisphere is slanted toward the sun, making the days longer and warmer than in winter. (2) Many religions make use of the solstices in their rites. (3) The first day of summer is called the *summer solstice* and is also the longest day of the year. (4) However, June 21 marks the beginning of winter in the southern hemisphere, when that hemisphere is tilted away from the sun.

333. a. Sentence 1
 b. Sentence 2
 c. Sentence 3
 d. Sentence 4

(1) People are quick to blame the weatherman if it rains on their parade! (2) The American Meteorological Society defines a meteorologist as a person "who uses scientific principles to explain, understand, observe, or forecast the earth's atmospheric phenomena and/or how the atmosphere affects the earth and life on the planet." (3) Many meteorologists have degrees in physics, chemistry, and other fields. (4) Their work often involves teaching, weather forecasting, atmospheric research, and other kinds of applied meteorology.

334. a. Sentence 1
 b. Sentence 2
 c. Sentence 3
 d. Sentence 4

(1) The park was empty, except for a child who stood just on the other side of the fence, a little girl about seven years old, thin and pale, with dark eyes and dark hair cut short and ragged. (2) The statistics on neglected children in our country probably fall short of the actual numbers. (3) The child wore no coat, only a brown, cotton skirt that was too big for her—pinned at the waist with a safety pin—and a soiled, long-sleeved yellow blouse with rhinestone buttons. (4) Her fingernails were dirty and broken, the tips of her fingers bluish with cold.

335. a. Sentence 1
 b. Sentence 2
 c. Sentence 3
 d. Sentence 4

(1) Ghosts can be either benevolent or malevolent. **(2)** As someone once said, "I don't believe in ghosts, but I'm afraid of them." **(3)** They can be comic and comfortable, like the old sea captain in *The Ghost and Mrs. Muir*, or horrific beyond belief, like the ghosts of the revelers at the party in the Overlook Hotel in Stephen King's *The Shining*. **(4)** They can emerge from the afterlife to teach us lessons, like old Marley in *A Christmas Carol*, or come back moaning to be avenged, like the ghost in *Hamlet*.

336. **a.** Sentence 1
b. Sentence 2
c. Sentence 3
d. Sentence 4

(1) There are many ways to benefit from a weight-lifting program. **(2)** Using light weights for many repetitions builds muscle tone and protects against injuries. **(3)** Using heavy weights for just a few repetitions builds muscle mass and makes the body stronger. **(4)** There are many gyms that provide personal trainers.

337. **a.** Sentence 1
b. Sentence 2
c. Sentence 3
d. Sentence 4

(1) C. S. Lewis is best known for his fantasy stories called *The Chronicles of Narnia*. **(2)** Lewis lived in Cambridge, England. **(3)** He was actually a prolific author, however, and wrote a great many books. **(4)** He was not limited to fantasy, but also wrote science fiction, satire, and many other types of literature.

338. **a.** Sentence 1
b. Sentence 2
c. Sentence 3
d. Sentence 4

(1) Ladders come in many shapes and sizes. **(2)** Aluminum ladders can conduct electricity, and should never be used near power lines. **(3)** Even wooden ladders, however, will conduct electricity. **(4)** The safest approach is to keep all ladders safely away from power lines.

339. a. Sentence 1
b. Sentence 2
c. Sentence 3
d. Sentence 4

(1) A book is actually a complicated item, composed of many parts. **(2)** The spine is what holds the book together, just as your spine enables you to stand upright. **(3)** Many people also enjoy buying used books. **(4)** The pages are like tongues, speaking words to the reader and communicating ideas.

340. a. Sentence 1
b. Sentence 2
c. Sentence 3
d. Sentence 4

(1) Firefighters must learn the proper procedures for responding to residential carbon monoxide (CO) emergencies. **(2)** Upon arriving at the scene of the alarm, personnel shall put on protective clothing and then bring an operational, calibrated CO meter onto the premises. **(3)** CO poisoning can be lethal, both to firefighters and to ordinary citizens. **(4)** Occupants of the premises shall then be examined, and if they are experiencing CO poisoning symptoms—i.e., headaches, nausea, confusion, dizziness, and other flu-like symptoms—an Emergency Medical Services (EMS) crew shall be sent immediately to evacuate and administer oxygen to the occupants.

341. a. Sentence 1
b. Sentence 2
c. Sentence 3
d. Sentence 4

SET 31 (Answers begin on page 180.)

For each of the following groups of three to four numbered sentences, choose the sentence order that would result in the best paragraph.

(1) Figures have the power to mislead people. **(2)** Mathematics tells us about economic trends, patterns of disease, and the growth of populations. **(3)** Math is good at exposing the truth, but it can also perpetuate misunderstandings and untruths.

342. **a.** 1, 2, 3
    b. 2, 3, 1
    c. 3, 1, 2
    d. 3, 2, 1

(1) The reason for so many injuries and fatalities is that a vehicle can generate heat of up to 1,500°F. **(2)** Firefighters know that the dangers of motor-vehicle fires are too often overlooked. **(3)** In the United States, 1 out of 5 fires involves motor vehicles, resulting each year in 600 deaths, 2,600 civilian injuries, and 1,200 injuries to firefighters.

343. **a.** 1, 2, 3
    b. 1, 3, 2
    c. 2, 3, 1
    d. 3, 2, 1

(1) There is no harm in putting a special treat in your child's lunch-box from time to time. **(2)** Usually, healthy snacks are defined as foods with low sugar and fat content. **(3)** Some examples include carrot and celery sticks, granola bars, yogurt drinks, and string cheese. **(4)** However, in general, it is a much better idea to provide healthy snacks.

344. **a.** 2, 4, 1, 3
    b. 1, 4, 2, 3
    c. 1, 2, 3, 4
    d. 3, 1, 2, 4

(**1**) Additionally, once a year, the association hosts a block party with food, music, and games. (**2**) The association organizes neighborhood watch teams and liaises with the police department on issues of crime and safety. (**3**) The main goal of the neighborhood association is to help make the community a safer place.

345. a. 1, 2, 3
b. 3, 2, 1
c. 2, 3, 1
d. 3, 1, 2

(**1**) Leaving us behind in a bitter cloud of exhaust, the bus would cough and jolt down the narrow main street of Crossland. (**2**) Then, even before the bus got moving, she'd look away, ahead toward her real life. (**3**) But I could always imagine the way it would be once it got out on the open highway, gathered speed, and took Grandma back to a life as exotic to me as the deserts of Egypt. (**4**) When Grandma's visit was over, we'd take her down to the Greyhound station, watch her hand her ticket to the uniformed driver, disappear inside, and reappear to wave goodbye—her expression obscured by the bus's grimy window.

346. a. 4, 2, 1, 3
b. 4, 1, 3, 2
c. 1, 3, 4, 2
d. 1, 2, 3, 4

(**1**) The Fifth Amendment of the U.S. Constitution guarantees citizens freedom from double jeopardy in criminal proceedings. (**2**) It also means a person cannot be tried for a crime for which he has already been convicted; that is to say, a person convicted by a state court cannot be tried for the same offense in, for example, federal court. (**3**) Finally, a person cannot be punished more than once for the same crime. (**4**) This means that a person cannot be tried for a crime for which he has already been acquitted.

347. a. 1, 4, 2, 3
b. 1, 2, 4, 3
c. 3, 2, 1, 4
d. 3, 4, 2, 1

(1) If these new policies are any indication, employees will have much less freedom than they did before. (2) The handbook also states that employees must give at least three weeks notice before taking a personal day. (3) The new employee handbook states that anyone who is out sick for more than three days must provide a doctor's note.

348. a. 2, 3, 1
  b. 3, 1, 2
  c. 3, 2, 1
  d. 1, 3, 2

(1) Every spring the softball field became his favorite destination; he had taken his son, Arnie, there when he was small to teach him how to pitch. (2) He walked home, as usual, through the park and, as usual, passed by the softball field. (3) This memory made him feel sad and guilty. (4) Arnie hadn't been in the least interested in softball, and so after two or three lessons, he had given up the idea.

349. a. 2, 1, 4, 3
  b. 3, 2, 1, 4
  c. 4, 3, 1, 2
  d. 2, 3, 4, 1

(1) If there are expenses incurred, complete report form 103; if there was damage to equipment, complete form 107. (2) If form 107 and form 103 are required, complete form 122 also. (3) Log on to the computer and go to the directory that contains the report forms. (4) As an employee, you must complete all paperwork.

350. a. 3, 2, 1, 4
  b. 1, 3, 4, 2
  c. 2, 1, 4, 3
  d. 4, 3, 1, 2

(1) In some areas, the salt is combined with calcium chloride, which is more effective in below-zero temperatures and which melts ice better. **(2)** After a snow or icefall, city streets are treated with ordinary rock salt. **(3)** This combination of salt and calcium chloride is also less damaging to foliage along the roadways.

351. a. 2, 1, 3
b. 1, 3, 2
c. 3, 2, 1
d. 2, 3, 1

(1) Yet the human brain is the most mysterious and complex object on Earth. **(2)** It has created poetry and music, planned and executed horrific wars, and devised intricate scientific theories. **(3)** It thinks and dreams, plots and schemes, and easily holds more information than all the libraries on Earth. **(4)** It weighs less than three pounds and is hardly more interesting to look at than an overly ripe cauliflower.

352. a. 1, 3, 4, 2
b. 2, 1, 4, 3
c. 3, 1, 2, 4
d. 4, 1, 2, 3

(1) Internal combustion engines traditionally required a carburetor to function correctly. **(2)** The carburetor was a small chamber where the gasoline vapors mixed with air. **(3)** Nowadays, however, fuel injection has made the carburetor obsolete. **(4)** Gasoline requires oxygen to burn, and without this mixture, the engine could not run.

353. a. 4, 3, 2, 1
b. 2, 4, 3, 1
c. 1, 2, 4, 3
d. 3, 2, 1, 4

(1) They are easy to plant and delightful to look at. (2) Irises, also called *flags*, are a colorful flower that grows in moist soil. (3) They are common all over the United States, and make a wonderful choice for any yard.

354. **a.** 3, 1, 2
      b. 2, 3, 1
      c. 2, 1, 3
      d. 1, 3, 2

(1) My friend Paul is an excellent example of reliability. (2) He always keeps his word, even when it becomes inconvenient or costly to him. (3) This is the secret of being reliable: do what you say you'll do, no matter what.

355. **a.** 1, 2, 3
      b. 2, 1, 3
      c. 2, 3, 1
      d. 3, 1, 2

SET 32 (Answers begin on page 182.)
Answer questions 356–358 on the basis of the following passage.

(1) Greyhound racing is the sixth most popular spectator sport in the United States. (2) Over the last decade, a growing number of racers have been adopted to live out retirement as household pets, once there racing career is over.

(3) Many people hesitate to adopt a retired racing greyhound because they think only very old dogs are available. (4) People also worry that the greyhound will be more nervous and active than other breeds and will need a large space to run. (5) _____. (6) In fact, racing greyhounds are put up for adoption at a young age; even champion racers, who have the longest careers, only work until they are about three-and-a-half years old. (7) Since greyhounds usually live to be 12–15 years old, their retirement is much longer than their racing careers. (8) Far from being nervous dogs, greyhounds have naturally sweet, mild dispositions, and, while they love to run, they are sprinters rather than distance runners and are sufficiently exercised with a few laps around a fenced-in backyard everyday.

(9) Greyhounds do not make good watchdogs, but they are very good with children, get along well with other dogs (and usually cats as well), and are very affectionate and loyal. (10) A retired racing greyhound is a wonderful pet for almost anyone.

356. Which sentence, if inserted in the blank space labeled Part 5, would best help to focus the writer's argument in the second paragraph?
    a. Even so, greyhounds are placid dogs.
    b. These worries are based on false impressions and are easily dispelled.
    c. Retired greyhounds do not need race tracks to keep in shape.
    d. However, retired greyhounds are too old to need much exercise.

357. Which of the following changes is needed in the first paragraph?
    a. Part 1: Change *growing* to *increasing*.
    b. Part 2: Change *there* to *their*.
    c. Part 1: Change *is* to *was*.
    d. Part 2: Change *have been adopted* to *have adopted*.

358. Which of the following sentences, if added between Parts 9 and 10 of the third paragraph, would be most consistent with the writer's purpose, tone, and intended audience?
    a. Former racing dogs make up approximately 0.36% of all dogs owned as domestic pets in the United States.
    b. Despite the fact that greyhounds make excellent domestic pets, there is still a large number of former racers who have not been adopted.
    c. Good-natured and tolerant dogs, greyhounds speedily settle into any household, large or small; they are equally at ease in an apartment or a private home.
    d. It is imperative that people overcome the common myths they harbor about greyhounds that are preventing them from adopting these gentle dogs.

Answer questions 359–361 on the basis of the following paragraph.

(1) Following an overwhelmingly enthusiastic response, the school administration has decided to expand the Community Mural Painting Program—now a part of two high school curriculums—to the middle school level. (2) The program was piloted in the school district last year and it was a successful initiative for students and for the community.

(3) Money to fund the program came from a national grant designed to promote community involvement as well as art appreciation among teenagers. (4) A committee that consists of art teachers, social studies teachers, and school social workers oversees the program.

(5) Studies have shown that young people who have been exposed to similar programs are much less prone to apathy. (6) The same studies state that these programs promote a sense of purpose that serves young people well both inside and outside the academic setting. (7) When the students were interviewed by the program committee. (8) In addition, the community attitude toward teenagers is improved also.

(9) It is projected that this year more than 150 students will be involved and that more than 20 murals will be painted.

359. Which sentence in the third paragraph is a nonstandard sentence?
  a. Part 5
  b. Part 6
  c. Part 7
  d. Part 8

360. Which of the following changes should be made to Part 8 of the passage?
  a. Remove the word *also*.
  b. Change *community* to *communities*.
  c. Change *teenagers* to *teenagers'*.
  d. Change *toward* to *according to*.

361. Which of the following sentences, if inserted after Part 2 of the passage, would best develop the ideas in the first paragraph?
   a. The program could benefit other districts as well.
   b. One particularly beautiful mural was painted on a playground wall on the east side of town.
   c. Fifty high school students were involved and they spent five weeks painting ten murals throughout the community in locations that were in great need of some attention.
   d. The school district is interested in trying other pilot programs in addition to the Mural Painting Program.

Answer questions 362 and 363 on the basis of the following passage.

(1) Yesterday I was exposed to what was called, in a recent newspaper ad for Dilly's Deli, "a dining experience like no other." (2) I decided on the hamburger steak special, the other specials were liver and onions and tuna casserole. (3) Each special is offered with two side dishes, but there was no potato salad left, and the green beans were cooked nearly beyond recognition. (4) I chose the gelatin of the day and what turned out to be the blandest coleslaw I have ever eaten.

(5) At Dilly's you sit at one of the four long tables. (6) The couple sitting across from me was having an argument. (7) The truck driver sitting next to me told me more than I wanted to know about highway taxes. (8) <u>After tasting</u> each of the dishes on my plate, it was time to leave; at that moment, one of the people working behind the counter yelled at me to clean up after myself. (9) Throwing away that plate of food was the most enjoyable part of dining at Dilly's.

362. Which of the following changes should be made to Part 2 of the first paragraph?
   a. Replace *were* with *are*.
   b. Replace the comma with a dash.
   c. Replace *I decided* with *Deciding*.
   d. Replace the comma with a semicolon.

363. Which of the following words or phrases should replace the underlined words in Part 8 of the second paragraph?
   a. Having tasted
   b. After I tasted
   c. Tasting
   d. After having tasted

SET 33 (Answers begin on page 184.)
Answer questions 364–366 on the basis of the following passage.

(**1**) Although eating right is an important part of good health, most experts agree that being physically active is also a key element in living a longer and healthier life. (**2**) The benefits of physical activity include improved self-esteem, a lowered risk of heart disease and colon cancer, stronger bones, muscles, and joints, and enhanced flexibility. (**3**) Physical activity, in addition to its many other rewards will also help manage weight gain.

(**4**) One of the simplest and most effective ways to increase physical activity are walking; walking requires no special equipment, no particular location, and it can be easily incorporated into even the busiest lives. (**5**) Add ten minutes or ten blocks to your usual dog-walking routine. (**6**) Park several blocks away from your destination and walk briskly the rest of the way. (**7**) Walk up or down the soccer or softball field while watching your kids play. (**8**) Find a walking buddy who will take a long walk with you once or twice a week. (**9**) You'll be less likely to skip the walk, if someone is counting on you to be there.

(**10**) _____. (**11**) Before long, it will become a normal part of your daily routine and you'll hardly notice the extra effort. (**12**) In addition, the increased energy and overall sense of well-being you'll experience will inspire you to walk even more.

364. Which of the following revisions is necessary in Part 4 of the above passage?

a. One of the simplest and most effective ways to increase physical activity are walking; walking requires no special equipment, no particular location and it can be easily incorporated into even the busiest lives.

b. One of the simplest and most effective ways to increase physical activity is walking; walking requires no special equipment, no particular location, and it can be easily incorporated into even the busiest lives.

c. One of the simplest and most effective ways to enhance physical activity are walking; walking requires no special equipment, no particular location, and it can be easily incorporated into even the busiest lives.

d. One of the simplest and most effective ways to increase physical activity are walking; only walking requires no special equipment, no particular location, and it can be easily incorporated into even the busiest lives.

365. Which of the following sentences, if inserted in the blank line numbered Part 10, would be most consistent with the development and grammar of the paragraph?

a. People will benefit from putting on their walking shoes and pounding the pavement.

b. So jog, bicycle, and walk as much as you can.

c. While people will benefit from increased physical activity, it cannot replace the necessity of eating right.

d. So put on your walking shoes and start pounding the pavement.

366. Which of the following changes is needed in the passage?

a. Part 3: Insert comma after *rewards*.

b. Part 1: Replace *most* with *more*.

c. Part 5: Insert a comma after *minutes*.

d. Part 2: Insert a colon after *activity*.

Answer questions 367 and 368 on the basis of the following passage.

(1) Police officers must read suspects their Miranda rights upon taking them into custody. (2) When a suspect who is merely being questioned <u>incriminates</u> himself, he might later claim to have been in custody and seek to have the case dismissed on the grounds of not having been <u>appraised</u> of his Miranda rights. (3) In such cases, a judge must make a determination as to whether or not a reasonable person would have believed himself to have been in custody, based on certain <u>criteria</u>. (4) Officers must be aware of these criteria and take care not to give suspects grounds for later claiming they believed themselves to be in custody. (5) The judge must <u>ascertain</u> whether the suspect was questioned in a threatening manner (threatening could mean that the suspect was seated while both officers remained standing) and whether the suspect was aware that he or she was free to leave at any time.

367. Which of the underlined words in the paragraph should be replaced by a more appropriate, accurate word?
   a. incriminates
   b. appraised
   c. criteria
   d. ascertain

368. Which of the following changes would make the sequence of ideas in the paragraph clearer?
   a. Place Part 5 after Part 1.
   b. Reverse Parts 3 and 5.
   c. Reverse the order of Parts 4 and 5.
   d. Delete Part 2.

Answer questions 369 and 370 on the basis of the following passage.

(1) Snowboarding, often described as a snow sport that combines skateboarding and surfing, is an increasingly common winter sport throughout the world. (2) Snowboarding involves strapping a board to one's feet and sliding down snow-covered mountains. (3) In addition to the snowboard, a snowboarder's equipment consists of special boots that attach to the board.

(**4**) Some find snowboarding more difficult to learn than skiing however, others consider it easier, requiring the mastery of one board as opposed to two skis and two poles. (**5**) All agree though, that once the sport is mastered, it is exciting, stimulating, and fun. (**6**) Those who excel in the sport may even find himself bound for the Olympics since snowboarding became medal-eligible in 1998.

369. Which of the following parts of the passage is a nonstandard sentence?
    a. Part 1
    b. Part 3
    c. Part 4
    d. Part 6

370. Which of the following changes is needed in the passage?
    a. Part 1: Change *combines* to *combine.*
    b. Part 2: Change *snow-covered* to *snow covered.*
    c. Part 5: Change *agree* to *agreed.*
    d. Part 6: Change *himself* to *themselves.*

Answer questions 371 and 372 on the basis of the following passage.

(**1**) Abraham Lincoln was the sixteenth president of the United States, and many Americans consider him to have been the greatest leader that the nation has yet produced. (**2**) He led the Nation through its most dangerous and tumultuous period, when the country was divided in two by the Civil War. (**3**) He also ended slavery in the United States, which no other leader had been able to accomplish.

(**4**) Lincoln was also a great orator, and gave many great speeches during his time in office. (**5**) Those speeches served to strengthen his position as a leader by motivating the American people to hold the nation together. (**6**) Lincoln is also honored on U.S. currency.

(**7**) Perhaps the most convincing proof of his greatness is the fact that Lincoln accomplished all this in only one term as president. (**8**) Abe Lincoln was assassinated shortly after being elected to his second term; one wonders what he might have accomplished had his life not been cut short.

371. Which of the following numbered parts is least relevant to the main idea of these paragraphs?

    a. Part 1

    b. Part 6

    c. Part 7

    d. Part 8

372. Which of the following changes is needed in the passage?

    a. Part 1: Place a comma after *Lincoln*.

    b. Part 3: Remove the comma after *States*.

    c. Part 2: Use a lowercase *n* for the word *Nation*.

    d. Part 4: Capitalize *orator*.

Answer questions 373–374 on the basis of the following passage.

(1) There are two types of diabetes, insulin-dependent and non-insulin-dependent. **(2)** Between 90 and 95% of the estimated 13 to 14 million people in the United States with diabetes have non-insulin-dependent, or Type II, diabetes. **(3)** Because this form of diabetes originally appeared in adults over the age of 40 and was most common after the age of 55, it used to be called *adult-onset* diabetes. This name is no longer appropriate, however, as an increasing number of young people—children included—are being diagnosed with the non-insulin-dependent form. **(4)** Nearly half of all people with diabetes do not know they have it, _____ its symptoms often develop gradually and are hard to identify at first. **(5)** _____ , someone who has developed Type II diabetes may feel more tired or ill without knowing why. **(6)** This can be particularly dangerous because untreated diabetes can cause damage to the heart, blood vessels, eyes, kidneys, and nerves. **(7)** While the causes, short-term effects, and treatments of the two types of diabetes differ, both types can cause the same long-term health problems.

373. Which of the following parts of the paragraph contains a nonstandard comparison?

    a. Part 7

    b. Part 5

    c. Part 3

    d. Part 2

374. Which sequence of words, if inserted in order into the blanks in the paragraph, help the reader understand the sequence and logic of the writer's ideas?
   a. since . . . For example
   b. while . . . Next
   c. moreover . . . Eventually
   d. because . . . Thus

SET 34 (Answers begin on page 186.)
Answer questions 375–377 on the basis of the following paragraph.

(1) By using tiny probes as neural prostheses, scientists may be able to restore nerve function in quadriplegics, make the blind see, or the deaf hear. (2) Thanks to advanced techniques, an implanted probe can stimulate individual neurons electrically or chemically and then record responses. (3) Preliminary results suggest that the microprobe telemetry systems can be permanently implanted and replace damaged or missing nerves.

(4) The tissue-compatible microprobes represent an advance over the typically aluminum wire electrodes used in studies of the cortex and other brain structures. (5) Previously, researchers data were accumulated using traditional electrodes, but there is a question of how much damage they cause to the nervous system. (6) Microprobes, since they are slightly thinner than a human hair, cause minimal damage and disruption of neurons when inserted into the brain because of their diminutive width.

(7) In addition to recording nervous system impulses, the microprobes have minuscule channels that open the way for delivery of drugs, cellular growth factors, neurotransmitters, and other neuroactive compounds to a single neuron or to groups of neurons. (8) The probes usually have up to four channels, each with its own recording/stimulating electrode.

375. Which of the following changes is needed in the above passage?
   a. Part 8: Change *its* to *it's*.
   b. Part 6: Change *their* to *its*.
   c. Part 6: Change *than* to *then*.
   d. Part 5: Change *researchers* to *researchers'*.

376. Which of the following includes a nonstandard use of an adverb in the passage?
   a. Part 2
   b. Part 4
   c. Part 6
   d. Part 8

377. Which of the following numbered parts should be revised to reduce unnecessary repetition?
   a. Part 2
   b. Part 5
   c. Part 6
   d. Part 8

Answer questions 378–380 on the basis of the following passage.

(1) Loud noises on trains not only irritate passengers but also create unsafe situations. (2) They are prohibited by law and by agency policy. (3) Therefore, conductors follow the procedures outlined below.

(4) A passenger-created disturbance is by playing excessively loud music or creating loud noises in some other manner. (5) In the event a passenger creates a disturbance, the conductor will politely ask the passenger to turn off the music or stop making the loud noise. (6) If the passenger refuses to comply, the conductor will tell the passenger that he or she is in violation of the law and train policy and will have to leave the train if he or she will not comply to the request. (7) If police assistance is requested, the conductor will stay at the location from which the call to the Command Center was placed or the silent alarm was used. (8) Conductors will wait there until the police arrive, will allow passengers to get off the train at this point, and no passengers are allowed back on board until the situation is resolved.

378. Which of the following numbered parts contains a nonstandard sentence?
   a. Part 3
   b. Part 4
   c. Part 6
   d. Part 7

379. Which of the following sentences is the best revision of the sentence numbered Part 8 in the passage?

    a. Conductors will wait there until the police arrive, will allow passengers off the train at this point, and no passengers will be allowed on until the situation is resolved.

    b. Conductors will wait there until the police arrive, will allow passengers off the train at this point, and, until the situation is resolved, no passengers are allowed on.

    c. Conductors will wait there until the police arrive, will allow passengers off the train at this point, and will not allow passengers back on board until the situation is resolved.

    d. Conductors will wait there until the police arrive, will allow passengers off the train at this point, and no passengers will be allowed on until the situation is resolved.

380. Which of the following numbered parts contains a nonstandard use of a preposition?

    a. Part 2

    b. Part 6

    c. Part 7

    d. Part 8

Answer questions 381–383 on the basis of the following passage.

(**1**) In her lecture "Keeping Your Heart Healthy," Dr. Miranda Woodhouse challenged Americans to join her in the fight to reduce the risks of heart disease. (**2**) Her plan includes four basic strategies meant to increase public awareness and prevent heart disease. (**3**) Eating a healthy diet that contains nine full servings of fruits and vegetables each day can help lower cholesterol levels. (**4**) More fruits and vegetables means less dairy and meat, which, in turn, means less cholesterol-boosting saturated fat. (**5**) Do not smoke. (**6**) Cigarette smoking which increases the risk of heart disease and when it is combined with other factors, the risk is even greater. (**7**) Smoking increases blood pressure, increases the tendency for blood to clot, decreases good cholesterol, and decreases tolerance for exercise. (**8**) Be aware of your blood pressure and cholesterol levels at all times. (**9**) Because their are often no symptoms, many people don't even know that they have high blood pressure. (**10**) This is extremely dangerous since uncontrolled high blood pressure can lead to heart attack, kidney failure, and stroke. (**11**) Finally, relax and be happy. (**12**) Studies show that being constantly angry and depressed can increase your risk of heart disease so take a deep breath, smile, and focus on the positive things in life.

381. Which of the following numbered parts contains a nonstandard sentence?
   a. Part 3
   b. Part 6
   c. Part 2
   d. Part 10

382. Which of the following sentences, if inserted between Part 2 and Part 3 of the passage, would best focus the purpose of the writer?
   a. While the guidelines will help those who are free of heart disease, they will not help those who have already experienced a heart attack.
   b. Extending the life of American citizens will make our country's life expectancy rates the highest in the world.
   c. The following is a brief outline of each of the four strategies.
   d. Getting people to stop smoking is the most important element of Dr. Woodhouse's program.

383. Which of the following changes needs to be made to the passage?
   a. Part 2: Change *includes* to *is inclusive of*.
   b. Part 3: Change *Eating* to *To eat*.
   c. Part 9: Change *their* to *there*.
   d. Part 12: Change *show* to *shown*.

Answer questions 384–387 on the basis of the following passage.

(**1**) Artist Mary Cassatt was born in Allegheny City, Pennsylvania, in 1844. (**2**) Because her family valued education and believed that traveling was a wonderful way to learn. (**3**) Before she was ten years old, she'd visited London, Paris, and Rome.

   (**4**) Although her family supported education, they were not at all supportive of her desire to be a professional artist but that didn't stop her from studying art both in the U.S. and abroad. (**5**) A contemporary of artists including Camille Pissarro and Edgar Degas Cassatt was an active member of the school of painting known as Impressionism. (6) However, in later years, her painting evolved and she abandoned the impressionist approach; for a simpler, more straightforward style.

(7) Cassatt never married or had children, but her most well-known painting's depict breathtaking, yet ordinary scenes of mothers and children. (8) Cassatt died in 1926 at the age of 82, leaving a large and inspired body of work and an example to women everywhere to break through traditional roles and follow their dreams.

384. Which of the following changes needs to be made to the above passage?
a. Part 3: Change *Before* to *Because*.
b. Part 4: Insert a comma after *Although*.
c. Part 5: Insert a comma after *Degas*.
d. Part 7: Change *breathtaking* to *breathtakingly*.

385. Which of the following numbered parts contains a nonstandard sentence?
a. Part 1
b. Part 2
c. Part 3
d. Part 8

386. Which of the following numbered parts contains a nonstandard sentence?
a. Part 3
b. Part 4
c. Part 6
d. Part 8

387. Which of the following should be used in place of the underlined word in Part 7 of the last paragraph?
a. painting
b. paintings
c. paintings'
d. artwork's

SET 35 (Answers begin on page 188.)
Answer questions 388–390 on the basis of the following passage.

(1) It is clear that the United States is a nation that needs to eat healthier and slim down. (2) One of the most important steps in the right <u>direction</u> would be for school cafeterias to provide healthy, low-fat options for students.

(3) School cafeterias, in an effort to provide food that is appetizing to young people, too often <u>memorize</u> fast-food menus, serving items such as burgers and fries, pizza, hot dogs, and fried chicken. (4) While these foods do provide some <u>nutritional</u> value, they are relatively high in fat. (5) According to nutritionist Elizabeth Warner, many of the lunch selections currently offered by school cafeterias could be made healthier with a few simple and inexpensive <u>substitutions.</u>

(6) "Veggie burgers offered alongside beef burgers would be a positive addition, says Warner. (7) "A salad bar would also serve the purpose of providing a healthy and satisfying meal. (8) And tasty grilled chicken sandwiches would be a far better option than fried chicken. (9) Additionally, the beverage case should be stocked with containers of low-fat milk."

388. Which of the following changes is needed in the third paragraph?
  a. Part 7: Remove the quotation marks before *A*.
  b. Part 6: Insert quotation marks after *addition,*.
  c. Part 9: Insert a comma after *case*.
  d. Part 8: Change *than* to *then*.

389. Which of the underlined words or phrases in the passage should be replaced by more precise or appropriate words?
  a. direction
  b. memorize
  c. nutritional
  d. substitutions

390. Which of the following editorial changes would help focus attention on the main idea in the third paragraph?
  a. Reverse the order of Part 7 and Part 9.
  b. Delete Part 6.
  c. Combine Part 7 and 8 into one sentence.
  d. Make Part 5 the first sentence of the third paragraph.

Answer questions 391–393 on the basis of the following passage.

(1) If you have little time to care for your garden, be sure to select hardy plants, such as phlox, comfrey, and peonies. (2) These will, with only a little care, keep the garden brilliant with color all through the growing season. (3) Sturdy sunflowers and hardy species of roses are also good selections. (4) As a thrifty gardener, you should leave part of the garden free for the planting of herbs such as lavender, sage, thyme, and parsley.

(5) If you have a moderate amount of time, growing vegetables and a garden culture of pears, apples, quinces, and other small fruits can be an interesting occupation, which amply rewards the care languished on it. (6) Even a small vegetable and fruit garden may yield radishes, celery, beans, and strawberries that will be delicious on the family table. (7) _____. (8) When planting seeds for the vegetable garden, you should be sure that they receive the proper amount of moisture, that they are sown at the right season to receive the right degree of heat, and that the seed is placed near enough to the surface to allow the young plant to reach the light easily.

391. Which of the following editorial changes would best help to clarify the ideas in the first paragraph?
   a. Omit the phrase, *with only a little care*, from Part 2.
   b. Reverse the order of Parts 2 and 3.
   c. Add a sentence after Part 4 explaining why saving room for herbs is a sign of thrift in a gardener.
   d. Add a sentence about the ease of growing roses after Part 3.

392. Which of the following sentences, if inserted in the blank line numbered Part 7, would be most consistent with the writer's development of ideas in the second paragraph?
   a. When and how you plant is important to producing a good yield from your garden.
   b. Very few gardening tasks are more fascinating than growing fruit trees.
   c. Of course, if you have saved room for an herb garden, you will be able to make the yield of your garden even more tasty by cooking with your own herbs.
   d. Growing a productive fruit garden may take some specialized and time-consuming research into proper grafting techniques.

393. Which of the following changes needs to be made in the above passage?
   a. Part 2: Change *through* to *threw*.
   b. Part 5: Change *languished* to *lavished*.
   c. Part 8: Change *sown* to *sewn*.
   d. Part 8: Change *surface* to *surfeit*.

Answer questions 394 and 395 on the basis of the following passage.

This selection is from Willa Cather's short story, "Neighbor Rosicky."

(1) On the day before Christmas the weather set in very cold; no snow, but a bitter, biting wind that whistled and sang over the flat land and lashed one's face like fine wires. (2) There was baking going on in the Rosicky kitchen all day, and Rosicky sat inside, making over a coat that Albert had outgrown into an overcoat for John. (3) Mary's big red geranium in bloom for Christmas, and a row of Jerusalem cherry trees, full of berries. (4) It was the first year she had ever grown these; Doctor Ed brung her the seeds from Omaha when he went to some medical convention. (5) They reminded Rosicky of plants he had seen in England; and all afternoon, as he stitched, he sat thinking about the two years in London, which his mind usually shrank from even after all this while.

394. Which of the following numbered parts displays nonstandard use of a verb form?
   a. Part 2
   b. Part 3
   c. Part 4
   d. Part 5

395. Which of the following numbered parts contains a nonstandard sentence?
   a. Part 2
   b. Part 3
   c. Part 4
   d. Part 5

SET 36 (Answers begin on page 189.)
Answer questions 396–398 on the basis of the following passage.

(1) Augustus Saint-Gaudens was born March 1, 1848, in Dublin, Ireland, to Bernard Saint-Gaudens, a French shoemaker, and Mary McGuinness, his Irish wife. (2) Six months later, the family immigrated to New York City, where Augustus grew up. (3) Upon completion of school at age thirteen, he expressed strong interest in art as a career so his father apprenticed him to a cameo cutter. (4) While working days at his cameo lathe, Augustus also took art classes at the Cooper Union and the National Academy of Design.

(5) At 19, his apprenticeship completed, Augustus traveled to Paris where he studied under Francois Jouffry at the renown Ecole des Beaux-Arts. (6) In 1870, he left Paris for Rome, where for the next five years, he <u>studies</u> classical art and architecture, and worked on his first commissions. (7) In 1876, he received his first major commission—a monument to Civil War Admiral David Glasgow Farragut. (8) Unveiled in New York's Madison Square in 1881, the monument was a tremendous success; its combination of realism and allegory was a departure from previous American sculpture. (9) Saint-Gaudens' fame grew, and other commissions were quickly forthcoming.

396. Which of the following numbered parts requires a comma to separate two independent clauses?
a. Part 1
b. Part 3
c. Part 7
d. Part 9

397. Which of the following words should replace the underlined word in Part 6?
a. studied
b. will study
c. had been studying
d. would have studied

398. Which of the following changes needs to be made to the passage?
   a. Part 2: Change *where* to *when*.
   b. Part 5: Change *renown* to *renowned*.
   c. Part 8: Change *its* to *it's*.
   d. Part 3: Change *expressed* to *impressed*.

Answer questions 399–401 on the basis of the following passage.

(1) Everglades National Park is the largest remaining sub-tropical wilderness in the continental United States. **(2)** It's home to abundant wildlife; including alligators, crocodiles, manatees, and Florida panthers. **(3)** The climate of the Everglades are mild and pleasant from December through April, though rare cold fronts may create near freezing conditions. **(4)** Summers are hot and humid; in summer, the temperatures often soar to around 90° and the humidity climbs to over 90%. **(5)** Afternoon thunderstorms are common, and mosquitoes are abundant. **(6)** If you visit the Everglades, wear comfortable sportswear in winter; loose-fitting, long-sleeved shirts and pants, and insect repellent are recommended in the summer.

(7) Walking and canoe trails, boat tours, and tram tours are excellent for viewing wildlife, including alligators and a multitude of tropical and temperate birds. **(8)** Camping, whether in the back country or at established campgrounds, offers the opportunity to enjoy what the park offers firsthand. **(9)** Year-round, ranger-led activities may help you to enjoy your visit even more; such activities are offered throughout the park in all seasons.

399. Which of the following numbered parts contains a nonstandard use of a semicolon?
   a. Part 6
   b. Part 2
   c. Part 9
   d. Part 4

400. Which of the following numbered parts needs to be revised to reduce unnecessary repetition?
   a. Part 4
   b. Part 6
   c. Part 9
   d. Part 8

401. Which of the following changes is needed in the above passage?
  a. Part 2: Change *it's* to *its*.
  b. Part 3: Change *are* to *is*.
  c. Part 6: Remove the comma after *Everglades*.
  d. Part 8: Remove the comma after *campgrounds*.

Answer questions 402 and 403 on the basis of the following passage.

(**1**) Choosing a doctor is an important decision. Here are some things you can do to make the best choice. (**2**) The single most important thing is to interview the doctors you are considering. (**3**) Ask questions about the practice, office hours, and how quick he or she responds to phone calls. (**4**) Pay attention to the doctor's communication skills and how comfortable you are with them. (**5**) The second thing you should do is to check the doctor's credentials. (**6**) One way to do this is to ask your health care insurance company how they checked the doctor's credentials before accepting him or her into their network. (**7**) The cost of healthcare insurance is quite high and many families have difficulty affording it. (**8**) Finally, spend a little time talking with the receptionist. (**9**) Keep in mind that this is the person you'll come into contact with every time you call or come into the office. (**10**) If he or she is pleasant and efficient, it will certainly make your overall experience better.

402. Which of the following numbered parts is least relevant to the first paragraph?
  a. Part 2
  b. Part 3
  c. Part 7
  d. Part 9

403. Which of the following changes needs to be made to the passage?
  a. Part 3: Change *quick* to *quickly*.
  b. Part 10: Change *better* to *more better*.
  c. Part 6: Change *accepting* to *accepted*.
  d. Part 10: Change *efficient* to *efficiently*.

Answer questions 404–406 on the basis of the following passage.

(1) Being able to type good is no longer a requirement limited to secretaries and novelists; thanks to the computer, anyone who wants to enter the working world needs to be <u>accustomed</u> to a keyboard. (2) Just knowing your way around a keyboard does not mean that you can use one efficiently, though; while you may have progressed beyond the "hunt-and-peck" method, you may never have learned to type quickly and accurately. (3) Doing so is a skill that will not only ensure that you pass a typing <u>proficiency</u> exam, but one that is essential if you want to advance your career in any number of fields. (4) This chapter <u>assures</u> that you are familiar enough with a standard keyboard to be able to use it without looking at the keys, which is the first step in learning to type, and that you are aware of the proper <u>fingering</u>. (5) The following information will help you increase your speed and accuracy and to do our best when being tested on timed writing passages.

404. Which of the following numbered parts contains a nonstandard use of a modifier?
   a. Part 1
   b. Part 2
   c. Part 3
   d. Part 5

405. Which of the following words, underlined in the passage, is misused in its context?
   a. assures
   b. proficiency
   c. fingering
   d. accustomed

406. Which of the following changes needs to be made in the passage?
   a. Part 3: Remove the comma after *exam*.
   b. Part 4: Insert a colon after *that*.
   c. Part 1: Change *needs* to *needed*.
   d. Part 5: Change *our* to *your*.

SET 37 (Answers begin on page 190.)
Answer questions 407 and 408 on the basis of the following passage.

(1) None of us knew my Uncle Elmer, not even my mother (he would have been ten years older than she) we had pictures of him in an ancient family album, a solemn, spindly baby, dressed in a white muslin shirt, ready for bed, or in a sailor suit, holding a little drum. (2) In one photograph, he stands in front of a tall chiffonier, which looms behind him, massive and shadowy, like one of the Fates in a greek play. (3) There weren't many such pictures, because photographs weren't easy to come by in those days, and in the ones we did have, my uncle had a formal posed look, as if, even then, he knew he was bound for some unique destiny. (4) It was the summer I turned thirteen that I found out what happened to him, the summer Sister Mattie Fisher, one of Grandma's evangelist friends, paid us a visit, sweeping in like a cleansing wind and telling the truth.

407. Which of the following changes needs to be made to the above passage?
   a. Part 2: Change *greek* to *Greek*.
   b. Part 4: Change *Sister* to *sister*.
   c. Part 4: Change *summer* to *Summer*.
   d. Part 3: Change *uncle* to *Uncle*.

408. Which of the following numbered parts contains a nonstandard sentence?
   a. Part 1
   b. Part 2
   c. Part 3
   d. Part 4

Answer questions 409–411 on the basis of the following passage.

(1) O'Connell Street is the main thoroughfare of Dublin City. (2) Although it is not a particularly long street Dubliners will tell the visitor proudly that it is the widest street in all of Europe. (3) This claim usually meets with protests, especially from French tourists who claim the Champs Elysées of Paris as Europe's widest street. (4) But the witty Dubliner will not <u>ensign</u> bragging rights easily and will trump the French visitor with a fine distinction: the Champs Elysées is the widest boulevard, but O'Connell is the widest street.

(5) Divided by several important monuments running the length of its center, the street is named for Daniel O'Connell, an Irish patriot. (6) An impressive monument to him towers over the entrance of lower O'Connell Street and overlooking the Liffey River. (7) O'Connell stands high above the unhurried crowds of shoppers, business people, and students on a sturdy column; he is surrounded by four serene angels seated at each corner of the monument's base.

409. Which of the following words should replace the underlined word in Part 4 of the passage?
   a. require
   b. relinquish
   c. acquire
   d. assign

410. Which of the following changes needs to be made to the second paragraph of the passage?
   a. Part 7: Replace the semicolon with a comma.
   b. Part 5: Change *Irish* to *irish*.
   c. Part 5: Change *running* to *run*.
   d. Part 6: Change *overlooking* to *overlooks*.

411. Which of the following changes needs to be made to the first paragraph of the passage?
   a. Part 2: Insert a comma after *that*.
   b. Part 3: Replace the comma after *protests* with a semicolon.
   c. Part 4: Remove the colon after *distinction*.
   d. Part 2: Insert a comma after *street*.

Answer questions 412–414 on the basis of the following passage.

(1) Mrs. Lake arriving twenty minutes early surprised and irritated Nicholas, although the moment for saying so slipped past too quickly for him to snatch its opportunity.

(2) She was a thin woman of medium height, not much older than he—in her middle forties he judged—dressed in a red-and-white, polka-dot dress and open-toed red shoes with extremely high heels. **(3)** Her short brown hair was crimped in waves, which gave a incongruous, quaint, old-fashioned effect. **(4)** She had a pointed nose. **(5)** Her eyes, set rather shallow, were light brown and inquisitive.

(6) "Dr. Markley?" she asked. **(7)** Nicholas nodded, and the woman walked in past him, proceeding with little mincing steps to the center of the living room where she stood with her back turned, looking around. **(8)** "My my," she said. **(9)** "This is a nice house. **(10)** Do you live here all alone?"

412. Which of the following changes should be made in Part 3?
  a. Change *was* to *is*.
  b. Change *gave* to *gives*.
  c. Change *a* to *an*.
  d. Change *effect* to *affect*.

413. Which of the following numbered parts contains a nonstandard use of a modifier?
  a. Part 7
  b. Part 5
  c. Part 3
  d. Part 2

414. Which of the following changes needs to be made to Part 1?
  a. Insert a comma after *early*.
  b. Change *too* to *two*.
  c. Change *Lake* to *Lake's*.
  a. Change *its* to *it's*.

SET 38 (Answers begin on page 191.)

Answer questions 415–417 on the basis of the following passage.

(1) If your office job involves telephone work, than your voice may be the first contact a caller has to your company or organization. (2) For this reason, your telephone manners have to be impeccable. (3) Always answer the phone promptly, on the first or second ring, if possible. (4) Speak directly into the phone, neither too loudly nor too softly, in a pleasant, cheerful voice. (5) Vary the pitch of your voice, so that it will not sound monotonous or uninterested, and be sure to enunciate clearly. (6) After a short, friendly greeting, state your company or boss's name, then your own name.

(7) Always take messages carefully. (8) Fill out all pertinent blanks on the message pad sheet while you are still on the phone. (9) Always let the caller hang up first. (10) Do not depend in your memory for the spelling of a name or the last digit of a phone number, and be sure to write legibly. (11) When it is time to close a conversation, do so in a pleasant manner, and never hang up without saying good-bye. (12) While it is not an absolute rule, generally closing with *goodbye* is more professional than *bye-bye*. (13) Verify the information by reading it back to the caller.

415. Which of the following editorial changes would most improve the clarity of development of ideas in the second paragraph?
   a. Delete Part 9.
   b. Reverse the order of Part 8 and Part 13.
   c. Reverse the order of Part 9 and Part 13.
   d. Add a sentence after Part 7 explaining the need to take phone messages from customers politely.

416. Which of the following changes needs to be made to the first paragraph?
   a. Part 5: Change *they* to *it*.
   b. Part 1: Change *than* to *then*.
   c. Part 2: Change *manners* to *manner*.
   d. Part 6: Change *boss's* to *bosses*.

417. Which of the following numbered parts contains a nonstandard use of a preposition?
a. Part 1
b. Part 2
c. Part 8
d. Part 10

Answer questions 418 and 419 on the basis of thefollowing passage.

(1) Understand that your boss has problems, too. (2) This is easy to forget. (3) When someone has authority over you, it's hard to remember that they're just human. (4) Your boss may have children at home who misbehave, dogs or cats or parakeets that need to go to the vet, deadlines to meet, and/or bosses of his or her own (sometimes even bad ones) overseeing his or her work. (5) If your boss is occasionally unreasonable, try to keep in mind that it might have nothing to do with you. (6) He or she may be having a bad day for reasons no one else knows. (7) Of course, if such behavior becomes consistently abusive, you'll have to do something about it—confront the problem or even quit. (8) But were all entitled to occasional mood swings.

418. Which of the following numbered parts contains a nonstandard use of a pronoun?
a. Part 3
b. Part 4
c. Part 7
d. Part 8

419. Which of the following changes needs to be made to the above passage?
a. Part 5: Change *unreasonable* to *unreasonably*.
b. Part 7: Change the dash to a semicolon.
c. Part 8: Change *were* to *we're*.
d. Part 4: Change *deadlines* to *a deadline*.

Answer questions 420 and 421 on the basis of the following passage.

(1) Patrick Henry is considered one of the great patriots of America's early history. **(2)** He was an early leader in every protest against British tyranny and in every movement for colonial rights, openly speaking against the unfair taxation and burdensome regulations imposed upon the American colonists by the British Parliament. **(3)** In March 1775, Patrick Henry urged his fellow Virginians to arm themselves in self-defense. **(4)** He spoke boldly in Richmond, Virginia, during the meeting of the state legislature. **(5)** He closes that famous speech with the immortal words, "I know not what course others may take; but as for me, give me liberty or give me death."

420. Which of the following sentences would be the best topic sentence for a second paragraph on the same subject?
   a. Patrick Henry was born on May 29, 1736, in Hanover County, Virginia.
   b. The Virginia legislature meets regularly from September through May every year.
   c. Taxes have gone up steadily in Virginia since the days of Patrick Henry.
   d. One rule of speechmaking is to speak clearly.

421. Which of the following numbered parts on the passage contains a wrong verb tense?
   a. Part 2
   b. Part 3
   c. Part 4
   d. Part 5

Answer questions 422 and 423 on the basis of the following passage.

(1) Beginning next month, City Transit will institute the Stop Here Program, who will be in effect every night from 10:00 p.m. until 4:00 a.m. **(2)** The program will allow drivers to stop the bus wherever a passenger wishes, as long as they deem it is safe to stop there. **(3)** This program will reduce the amount of walking that passengers will have to do after dark. **(4)** Passengers may request a stop anywhere along the bus route by pulling the bell cord a block ahead. **(5)** During the first two months of the program, when passengers attempt to flag down a bus anywhere but at a designated stop, the bus driver should proceed to the next stop and wait for them to board the bus. **(6)** Then the driver should give the passenger a brochure that explains the Stop Here Program.

422. Which of the following editorial changes in the above passage would best help to clarify the information the paragraph intends to convey?
   a. Add a sentence between Parts 4 and 5 explaining that while the Stop Here Program allows passengers to leave the bus at almost any point, passengers may board only at designated stops.
   b. Delete Part 6.
   c. Add a sentence between Parts 5 and 6 explaining the safety advantages for passengers of flagging down buses at night.
   d. Reverse the order of Parts 4 and 5.

423. Which of the following numbered parts contains a nonstandard use of a pronoun?
   a. Part 1
   b. Part 2
   c. Part 3
   d. Part 5

Answer questions 424 and 425 on the basis of the following passage.

(1) Last October, a disastrous wildfire swept across portions of Charlesburg. **(2)** Five residents were killed, 320 homes destroyed, and 19,500 acres burned. **(3)** A public safety task force was formed to review emergency choices. **(4)** The task force findings were as follows;

(5) The water supply in the residential areas was insufficient, some hydrants could not even be opened. **(6)** The task force recommended a review of hydrant inspection policy.

(7) The fire companies that responded had difficulty locating specific sites. **(8)** Most companies came from other areas and were not familiar with Miller Point. **(9)** The available maps were outdated and did not reflect recent housing developments.

(10) Evacuation procedures were inadequate. **(11)** Residents reported being given conflicting and/or confusing information. **(12)** Some residents of the Hilltop Estates subdivision ignored mandatory evacuation orders, yet others were praised for their cooperation.

424. Which of the following numbered parts contains a nonstandard sentence?
   a. Part 7
   b. Part 5
   c. Part 3
   d. Part 12

425. Which of the following changes needs to be made to the passage?
   a. Part 12: Change *were* to *we're*.
   b. Part 12: Insert a comma after *others*.
   c. Part 2: Remove the comma after *killed*.
   d. Part 4: Replace the semicolon with a colon.

SET 39 (Answers begin on page 193.)
Answer questions 426–428 on the basis of the following passage.

(1) In the early 1700s, sailors had no way of accurately <u>figure out</u> longitude. (2) They were able to estimate quite accurately what their Latitude was at any given time, but the instruments that they used could not ascertain longitude. (3) This created a very significant problem in navigation, as ship captains had to estimate their location by celestial navigation, <u>using</u> the stars and moon and other heavenly bodies to know where on Earth they were at any given time.

(4) A small error in their calculations could cause a ship to <u>reach</u> land hundreds of miles away from where the captain wanted to be. (5) During times of war, this problem could be catastrophic, as a ship might arrive at an enemy port rather than a friendly one.

(6) The problem was solved by an uneducated clockmaker named John Harrison. (7) Harrison invented a small clock that looked like an overgrown pocket watch, which he calls a chronometer. (8) This complex clock enabled ship captains to accurately determine their location at sea, and <u>remained</u> in use until the recent invention of modern satellite navigational systems.

426. Which of the underlined words in the passage could be replaced with a more precise verb?
   a. figure out
   b. using
   c. reach
   d. remained

427. Which of the following sentences uses the verb incorrectly?
   a. Part 3
   b. Part 5
   c. Part 7
   d. Part 2

428. Which of the following changes needs to be made in the passage?
   a. Part 2: Do not capitalize *Latitude.*
   b. Part 3: Capitalize *navigation.*
   c. Part 5: Remove the comma after *war.*
   d. Part 7: Add a comma after *clock.*

Answer questions 429 and 430 on the basis of the following passage.

(1) The ballpoint pen was invented in 1938 by a Hungarian named Laszlo Biro, a journalist who wanted a reliable pen that didn't leak unlike the fountain pens that were popularly used at the time. **(2)** Biro noticed that the ink used by his employer's to print newspapers dried very quickly, and he decided that it would be useful in a pen. **(3)** The problem was that newspaper ink was too thick to use in fountain pens; Biro needed to find another way to flow that ink onto paper.

   (4) His solution was to use a tiny steel ball in the tip of a pen nib. **(5)** The ball rotated inside its collar, picking up ink from the pen and transferring it smoothly onto paper. **(6)** The result was the ballpoint pen, which still bears the name of Biro in many European countries today.

429. Which of the following corrections should be made in punctuation?
   a. Part 2: Remove the apostrophe from *employer's.*
   b. Part 3: Change the semicolon to a comma.
   c. Part 5: Remove the comma after *collar.*
   d. Part 6: Change the comma to a semicolon.

430. Which of the following changes needs to be made in the first sentence?
   a. Add an apostrophe to *pens.*
   b. Add a comma after *leak.*
   c. Capitalize *ballpoint pen.*
   d. No changes need to be made.

Answer questions 431 and 432 on the basis of the following passage.

(1) Theodore Roosevelt <u>were</u> born with asthma and poor eyesight. (2) Yet this sickly child later won fame as a political leader, Rough Rider, and hero of the common people. (3) To conquer his handicaps, Teddy trained in a gym and became a lightweight boxer at Harvard. (4) Out west, he hunted buffalo and ran a cattle ranch. (5) He was civil service reformer in the east and also a police commissioner. (6) He became President McKinley's Assistant Naval Secretary during the Spanish-American War. (7) Also, he led a charge of cavalry Rough Riders up San Juan Hill in Cuba. (8) After achieving fame, he became Governor of New York and went on to become the Vice-President.

431. Which of the following sentences represents the best revision of Part 5?
   a. Back east, he became a civil service reformer and police commissioner.
   b. A civil service reformer and police commissioner was part of his job in the east.
   c. A civil service reformer and police commissioner were parts of his job in the east.
   d. His jobs of civil service reformer and police commissioner were his jobs in the east.

432. Which of the following should be used in place of the underlined verb in Part 1 of the passage?
   a. will be
   b. are
   c. is
   d. was

Answer questions 433–435 on the basis of the following passage.

(1) Charles Dickens was the most widely read author of the Victorian era, and one of the most prolific writers of modern times. (2) His novels remain popular even today because they present pictures of ordinary people facing extraordinary difficulties, people who have to deal with things that are hard and unusual, especially regular people

like you and me. **(3)** He is still so popular, in fact, that none of his novels has ever gone out of print, and all are still widely available today in inexpensive paperback editions.

(4) _____ **(5)** Many of those characters are memorable simply because of their peculiar characteristics, such as the eccentric but loveable traveler, Samuel Pickwick. **(6)** Other characters are famous largely because of Dickens' skill at giving them unusual names, such as Uriah Heep and Mr. Micawber.

(7) The novels tend to be long, but most readers are so drawn in by the stories that they are disappointed when the book ends. **(8)** These alone is a testimony to Dickens' skill as a storyteller.

433. Which of the following sentences would be most consistent with the passage's development if it were inserted into the blank in Part 4?
   a. Dickens' novels contain many memorable characters—people who come alive from the pages and remain in the minds of readers.
   b. Dickens' novels are available in paperback at your local bookstore.
   c. The novels address many themes, including poverty and pollution.
   d. Most of Dickens' novels include humorous incidents—things that are designed to make a reader laugh even in the midst of dark and serious details.

434. Which of the following numbered parts should be revised to reduce its unnecessary repetition?
   a. Part 6
   b. Part 5
   c. Part 2
   d. Part 1

435. Which of the following changes should be made in the final sentence (Part 8)?
   a. Change *skill* to *weakness.*
   b. Change *Dickens'* to *Dicken's.*
   c. Change *is* to *was.*
   d. Change *These* to *This.*

SET 40 (Answers begin on page 194.)

Answer questions 436–438 on the basis of the following passage.

(1) As soon as she sat down on the airplane, Rachel almost began to regret telling the travel agent that she wanted an exotic and romantic vacation; after sifting through a stack of brochures, the agent and her decided the most exotic vacation she could afford was a week in Rio. (2) As the plane hurtled toward Rio de Janeiro, she read the information on Carnival that was in the pocket of the seat in front of hers. (3) The very definition made her shiver: "from the Latin carnavale, meaning a farewell to the flesh." (4) She was searching for excitement, but had no intention of bidding her skin good-bye. (5) "Carnival," the brochure informed her, originated in Europe in the Middle Ages and served as a break from the requirements of daily life and society. (6) Most of all, it allowed the hard-working and desperately poor serfs the opportunity to ridicule their wealthy and normally humorless masters." (7) Rachel, a middle manager in a computer firm, wasn't entirely sure whether she was a serf or a master. (8) Should she be making fun, or would others be mocking her? (9) She was strangely relieved when the plane landed, as though her fate were decided.

436. Which of the following changes needs to be made to the above passage?
  a. Part 2: Insert *the* before *Carnival*.
  b. Part 3: Italicize *carnavale*.
  c. Part 6: Italicize *serfs*.
  d. Part 9: Change *were* to *was*.

437. Which of the following numbered parts contains a nonstandard use of a pronoun?
  a. Part 1
  b. Part 5
  c. Part 7
  d. Part 8

438. Which of the following changes needs to be made to Part 5 of the passage?
  a. Insert quotation marks before *originated*.
  b. Remove the comma after *her*.
  c. Remove the quotation marks around *Carnival*.
  d. Insert quotation marks around *society*.

Answer questions 439–441 on the basis of the following passage.

(1) A metaphor is a poetic device that deals with comparison. (2) It compares similar qualities of two dissimilar objects. (3) With a simple metaphor, one object becomes the other: *Love is a rose*. Although this doesn't sound like a particularly rich image, a metaphor can communicate so much about a particular image that poets utilize them more than any other type of figurative language. (4) The reason for this is that a poet composes poetry to express emotional experiences. (5) Succinctly, what the poet imagines love to be may or may not be our perception of love. (6) Therefore, the poet's job is to enable us to *experience* and feel it the same way. (7) You should be able to nod in agreement and say, "Yes, that's it! (8) I understand precisely where this guy is coming from."

439. The tone of this passage is very formal; the last sentence is not. Which of the following would be more consistent with the tone of the passage?
    a. This guy is right on.
    b. I can relate to the poet's experience.
    c. I know this feeling.
    d. This poem gets right to the point.

440. Which of the following numbered parts contains a nonstandard use of a pronoun?
    a. Part 3
    b. Part 5
    c. Part 6
    d. Part 7

441. Which of the following adverbs should replace the underline word in Part 5 of the passage?
    a. Consequently
    b. Normally
    c. Occasionally
    d. Originally

Answer questions 442–444 on the basis of the following passage.

(1) Light pollution a growing problem worldwide. (2) Like other forms of pollution, light pollution degrades the quality of the environment. (3) Where once it was possible to look up at the night sky and see thousands of twinkling stars in the inky blackness, one now sees little more than the yellow glare of urban sky glow. (4) When we lose the ability to connect visually with the vastness of the universe by looking up at the night sky, we lose our connection with something profoundly important to the human spirit—my sense of wonder.

442. Which of the endings to the following sentence would be the best concluding sentence for this passage? The most serious damage resulting from light pollution is to our
  a. artistic appreciation.
  b. sense of physical well-being.
  c. spiritual selves.
  d. cultural advancement.

443. Which of the following changes needs to be made to Part 4 of the passage?
  a. Change *we* to *you*.
  b. Change *my* to *our*.
  c. Change *we* to *I*.
  d. Change *my* to *his*.

444. Which of the following numbered parts contains a nonstandard sentence?
  a. Part 1
  b. Part 2
  c. Part 3
  d. Part 4

SET 41 (Answers begin on page 194.)
Answer questions 445–447 on the basis of the following passage.

(1) Typically people think of genius, whether it manifests itself in Mozart symphonies or Einstein's discovery of relativity, as having a quality not just of the divine, but also of the eccentric. (2) People see genius as a "good" abnormality; moreover, they think of genius as a completely unpredictable abnormality. (3) Until recently, psychologists regarded the quirks of genius as too erratic to describe intelligibly; however, Anna Findley's groundbreaking study uncovers predictable patterns in the biographies of geniuses. (4) Despite the regularity of these patterns, they could still support the common belief that there is a kind of supernatural intervention in the lives of unusually talented men and women. (5) _____. (6) For example, Findley shows that all geniuses experience three intensely productive periods in their lives, one of which always occurs shortly before their deaths; this is true whether the genius lives to nineteen or ninety.

445. Which of the following sentences, if inserted in the blank numbered Part 5, would best focus the main idea of the passage?
   a. These patterns are normal in the lives of all geniuses.
   b. Eerily, the patterns themselves seem to be determined by predestination rather than mundane habit.
   c. No matter how much scientific evidence the general public is presented with, people still like to think of genius as unexplainable.
   d. Since people think of genius as a "good" abnormality, they do not really care what causes it.

446. Which of the following changes needs to be made to the passage?
   a. Part 1: Change *Mozart* to *Mozart's*.
   b. Part 3: Change *too* to *to*.
   c. Part 4: Change *there* to *their*.
   d. Part 6: Change *geniuses* to *geniuses'*.

447. Which of the following numbered parts contains a nonstandard use of a pronoun?
   a. Part 2
   b. Part 3
   c. Part 4
   d. Part 6

Answer questions 448–450 on the basis of the following passage.

(1) Horatio Hornblower, a British naval hero whose exploits take place during the great age of sailing ships, is a fictional character created by author C. S. Forester. (2) The Hornblower novels trace the heros career from its very beginning, when he joins a British warship as a seasick midshipman, and follow his rise through the ranks until he reaches the level of Admiral of the Fleet.

(3) The Hornblower novels are famous for their exciting battle scenes, as wooden sailing ships range the seas firing broadsides at one another. (4) But these novels are significant for more than that: they also provide a very accurate picture of what life is like aboard those great ships of war during the eighteenth and nineteenth centuries. (5) It was a hard life! (6) Sailors lacked what we would consider edible food and drinkable water, often for months at a time. (7) Discipline was severe—a sailor could be flogged for what we today would consider minor offenses—yet the Hornblower novels also help us to understand that such discipline and self-denial were essential to the safety and effectiveness of warships in that age. (8) The Hornblower books are available in paperback and hardcover.

(9) Forester's Horatio Hornblower novels thus serve two very valuable functions: they give modern audiences a glimpse into a bygone era, showing us what life was like for the fighting men of the seas; and they manage to provide many hours of enjoyable reading in the process. (10) Combining these two elements together is indeed a remarkable literary feat.

448. Which of the following editorial changes should be made to improve the focus of the passage?
   a. Reverse the order of Parts 2 and 3.
   b. Remove Part 5.
   c. Part 10: Change *Combining* to *Combined.*
   d. Remove Part 8.

449. Which of the following changes needs to be made to the passage?
   a. Part 4: Add a comma after *But*
   b. Part 6: Remove the comma after *water*
   c. Part 2: Change *heros* to *hero's*
   d. Part 9: Change *Forester's* to *Foresters*

450. Which of the following sentences has an error in verb tense?
    a. Part 2
    b. Part 3
    c. Part 4
    d. Part 5

Answer questions 451–452 on the basis of the following passage.

(1) *The Disasters of War* is a famous series of prints by Spanish artist Francisco Goya, which he etched between 1810 and 1820. **(2)** The individual prints depict the devastating effects of the war waged by Napoleon against the people of Spain. **(3)** The scenes that the artist represented showed the ravages of the Napoleonic Wars on ordinary people focusing on the side effects various battles had on commoners.

    (4) This approach to artistic representation of battle was unusual at the time, since most artists sought to capture the actions and deeds of soldiers who were actually fighting the war. **(5)** But Goya wanted to protest against Napoleon's war-mongering and greed, so he showed the world what the battles did to ordinary people who were merely trying to live out their lives.

    (6) Goya feared that his prints would be very controversial, and that he might suffer for making them. **(7)** This fear caused him to keep the works secret not permitting them to be made public until well after his death.

451. In which of the following numbered parts should a comma be inserted?
    a. Part 6
    b. Part 7
    c. Part 1
    d. Part 2

452. Which of the following sentences is a run-on?
    a. Part 6
    b. Part 5
    c. Part 4
    d. Part 3

Answer questions 453–455 on the basis of the following passage.

(1) Whether or not you can accomplish a specific goal or meet a specific deadline depends first on how much time you need to get the job done. **(2)** What should you do when the demands of the job <u>precede</u> the time you have available. **(3)** The best approach is to correctly divide the project into smaller pieces. **(4)** Different goals will have to be divided in different ways, but one seemingly unrealistic goal can often be accomplished by working on several smaller, more reasonable goals.

453. Which of the following sentences has an error in the verb infinitive?
   a. Part 1
   b. Part 2
   c. Part 3
   d. Part 4

454. Which of the following words should replace the underlined word in Part 2 of the passage?
   a. exceed
   b. succeed
   c. supercede
   d. proceed

455. Which of the following sentences in the passage needs a question mark?
   a. Part 1
   b. Part 2
   c. Part 3
   d. Part 4

SET 42 (Answers begin on page 195.)
Answer questions 456 and 457 on the basis of the following passage.

(1) The Competitive Civil Service system is designed to give candidates fair and equal treatment and ensure that federal applicants are hired based on objective criteria. **(2)** Hiring has to be based solely on a candidate's knowledge, skills, and abilities (which you'll sometimes see abbreviated as KSA), and not on external factors such as race, religion, sex, and so on. **(3)** Whereas employers in the private sector can hire employees for subjective reasons, federal employers must be able to justify his decision with objective evidence that the candidate is qualified.

456. Which of the following sentences lacks parallelism?
   a. Part 1
   b. Part 2
   c. Part 3
   d. Parts 2 and 3

457. Which of the following sentences has an error in pronoun agreement?
   a. Part 1
   b. Part 2
   c. Part 3
   d. Parts 2 and 3

Answer questions 458 and 459 on the basis of the following passage.

(1) A light rain was falling. **(2)** He drove home by his usual route. **(3)** It was a drive he had taken a thousand times; still, he did not know why, as he passed the park near their home, he should so suddenly and vividly picture the small pond that lay at the center of it. **(4)** In winter, this pond was frozen over, and he had taken his daughter Abigail there when she was small and tried to teach her how to skate. **(5)** She hadn't been able to catch on, and so after two or three lessons Abigail and him had given up on the idea. **(6)** Now there came into his mind an image of such clarity it caused him to draw in his breath sharply; an image of Abigail gliding toward him on her new Christmas skates, going much faster than she should have been.

458. Which of the following changes needs to be made to the passage?
   a. Part 3: Change the semicolon to a comma.
   b. Part 4: Remove the word *and*.
   c. Part 5: Change the comma to a semicolon.
   d. Part 6: Change the semicolon to a colon.

459. Which of the following changes needs to be made to the passage?
   a. Part 3: Replace *their* with *there*.
   b. Part 4: Remove the comma after *over*.
   c. Part 5: Change *him* to *he*.
   d. Part 6: Replace *Christmas* with *Christmas'*.

Answer questions 460–462 on the basis of the following passage.

(1) For years, Mt. Desert Island, particularly its major settlement, Bar Harbor, afforded summer homes for the wealthy. **(2)** Finally though, Bar Harbor has become a burgeoning arts community as well. **(3)** But, the best part of the island is the unspoiled forest land known as Acadia National Park. **(4)** Since the island sits on the boundary line between the temperate and sub-Arctic zones the island supports the flora and fauna of both zones as well as beach, inland, and alpine plants. **(5)** Lies in a major bird migration lane and is a resting spot for many birds. **(6)** The establishment of Acadia National Park in 1916 means that this natural monument will be preserved and that it will be available to all people, not just the wealthy. **(7)** Visitors to Acadia may receive nature instruction from the park naturalists as well as enjoy camping, hiking, cycling, and boating. **(8)** Or they may choose to spend time at the archeological museum learning about the Stone Age inhabitants of the island.

460. Which of the following sentences is a sentence fragment?
   a. Part 2
   b. Part 3
   c. Part 4
   d. Part 5

461. Which of the following adverbs should replace the words *Finally though* in Part 2?
   a. Suddenly
   b. Concurrently
   c. Simultaneously
   d. Recently

462. Which of the following changes needs to be made to Part 4?
   a. Insert a comma after the word *zones*.
   b. Delete the word *Since* at the beginning of the sentence.
   c. Delete the comma after the word *inland*.
   d. Add a question mark at the end of the sentence.

Answer questions 463 and 464 on the basis of the following passage.

(1) A smoke detector should be placed on each floor level of a home and outside each sleeping area. (2) A good site for a detector would be a hallway that runs between living spaces and bedrooms.

   (3) Because of the "dead" air space that might be missed by turbulent hot air bouncing around above a fire, smoke detectors should be installed either at the ceiling at least four inches from the nearest wall, or high on a wall at least four, but no further than twelve, inches from the ceiling. (4) Detectors should not be mounted near windows, exterior doors, or other places where drafts might direct the smoke away from the unit. (5) Also, it should not be placed in kitchens and garages, where cooking and gas fumes are likely to set off false alarms.

463. Which of the following numbered parts contains a nonstandard use of a preposition?
   a. Part 1
   b. Part 3
   c. Part 4
   d. Part 5

464. In which of the following numbered parts should a pronoun be replaced with a different pronoun?
   a. Part 1
   b. Part 2
   c. Part 3
   d. Part 5

Answer questions 465–467 on the basis of the following passage.

(1) Heat exhaustion, generally characterized by clammy skin, fatigue, nausea, dizziness, profuse perspiration, and sometimes fainting, resulting from an inadequate intake of water and the loss of fluids. **(2)** First aid treatment for this condition includes having the victim lie down, raising the feet 8 to 12 inches, applying cool, wet cloths to the skin, and giving the victim sips of salt water (1 teaspoon per glass, half a glass every 15 minutes) over the period of an hour. **(3)** _____.

    (4) Heatstroke is much more serious; it is an immediate life-threatening condition. **(5)** The characteristics of heatstroke are a high body temperature (which may reach 106°F or more); a rapid pulse; hot, dry skin; and a blocked sweating mechanism. **(6)** Victims of this condition may be unconscious, and first aid measures should be directed at cooling the body quickly. **(7)** Heatstroke often occurs among poor people in urban areas. **(8)** The victim should be placed in a tub of cold water or repeatedly sponged with cool water until his or her temperature is lowered sufficiently. **(9)** Fans or air conditioners will also help with the cooling process. **(10)** Care should be taken, however, not to chill the victim too much once his or her temperature is below 102°F.

465. Which of the following sentences, if inserted into the blank in Part 3 in the passage, would best aid the transition of thought between the first and second paragraphs?
  a. Heat exhaustion is a relatively unusual condition in northern climates.
  b. The typical victims of heatstroke are the poor and elderly who cannot afford air conditioning even on the hottest days of summer.
  c. Heat exhaustion is never fatal, although it can cause damage to internal organs if it strikes an elderly victim.
  d. Air conditioning units, electric fans, and cool baths can lower the number of people who suffer heatstroke each year in the United States.

466. Which of the following numbered parts draws attention away from the main idea of the second paragraph of the passage?
   a. Part 6
   b. Part 7
   c. Part 8
   d. Part 10

467. Which of the following numbered parts contains a nonstandard sentence?
   a. Part 1
   b. Part 3
   c. Part 5
   d. Part 8

SET 43 (Answers begin on page 197.)
Answer questions 468 and 469 on the basis of the following passage.

(1) To test for carbon monoxide (CO) contamination, meters must be held head high. (2) Appliances should be operating for five to ten minutes before testing, a check must be made near all gas appliances and vents. (3) If vents are working properly, no CO emissions will enter the structure.

   (4) If the meters register unsafe levels—above 10 parts per million (ppm)—all occupants should be evacuated and the source of the contamination investigated. (5) Occupants should be interviewed to ascertain the location of the CO detector (if any), the length of time the alarm has sounded, what the occupants been doing at the time of the alarm, and what electrical appliances were functioning. (6) Occupants should not re-enter the premises until the environment is deemed safe.

468. Which of the following numbered parts contains a nonstandard verb form?
   a. Part 2
   b. Part 3
   c. Part 5
   d. Part 6

469. Which of the following numbered parts contains a nonstandard sentence?
   a. Part 2
   b. Part 4
   c. Part 5
   d. Part 6

Answer questions 470 and 471 on the basis of the following passage.

(1) Glaciers consist of fallen snow that compresses over many years into large, thickened ice masses. (2) Most of the world's glacial ice is found in Antarctica and Greenland glaciers are found on nearly every continent, even Africa. (3) Presently, 10% of land area is covered with glaciers. (4) Glacial ice often appears blue because ice absorbs all other colors but reflects blue. (5) Almost 90% of an iceberg is below water; only about 10% shows above water. (6) What makes glaciers unique is their ability to move? (7) Due to sheer mass, glaciers flow like very slow rivers. (8) Some glaciers are as small as football fields, while others grow to be over a hundred kilometers long.

470. Which of the following sentences is a run-on sentence?
   a. Part 1
   b. Part 2
   c. Part 3
   d. Part 4

471. Which of the following sentences contains an error in punctuation?
   a. Part 3
   b. Part 4
   c. Part 5
   d. Part 6

Answer question 472 on the basis of the following short description.

> **(1)** Herbert was enjoying the cool, bright fall afternoon. **(2)** Walking down the street, red and yellow leaves crunched satisfyingly under his new school shoes.

472. Which of the following is the best revision of the description?
   a. Herbert was enjoying the cool bright fall afternoon. Walking down the street red and yellow leaves crunched satisfyingly under his new school shoes.
   b. Herbert was enjoying the cool, bright fall afternoon. He was walking down the street, red and yellow leaves crunched satisfyingly under his new school shoes.
   c. Herbert was enjoying the cool, bright fall afternoon. Walking down the street, he crunched red and yellow leaves satisfyingly under his new school shoes.
   d. Herbert was enjoying the cool, bright fall afternoon. Walking down the street, red and yellow leaves were crunched satisfyingly under his new school shoes.

Answer questions 473–475 on the basis of the following passage.

> **(1)** The building in which Howard Davis was to teach his undergraduate evening course, Interpretation of Poetry, was Renwick Hall, the General Sciences Building. **(2)** Markham Hall, which housed the English Department offices and classrooms, was to be closed all summer for renovation.
>
> **(3)** Howard's classroom was in the basement. **(4)** The shadowy corridor that <u>led</u> back to it was lined with glass cases containing exhibits whose titles <u>read</u> *Small Mammals of North America*, *Birds of the Central United States*, and *Reptiles of the Desert Southwest*. **(5)** The dusty specimens perched on little stands; <u>their</u> tiny claws gripped the smooth wood nervously. **(6)** A typewritten card, yellow with age, bearing the name of its genus and species. **(7)** The classroom itself was outfitted with a stainless steel sink, and behind the lectern loomed a dark-wood cabinet through whose glass doors one could see rows of jars, each holding what appeared to be an animal embryo floating in a murky liquid. **(8)** The classroom <u>wreaked</u> of formaldehyde.

473. Which of the following sentences, if inserted between Parts 6 and 7, would best fit the author's pattern of development in the second paragraph of the passage?
   a. Howard would be teaching Byron, Shelley, and Keats this term.
   b. In the display case opposite Howard's classroom, a pocket gopher reared up on its hind legs, staring glassy-eyed into the open doorway.
   c. Although Markham was at least twenty-five years younger than Renwick, the administration had chosen to renovate it rather than the aging, crumbling science building.
   d. Genus and species are taxonomic categories.

474. Which of the following numbered parts contains a nonstandard sentence?
   a. Part 1
   b. Part 2
   c. Part 6
   d. Part 7

475. Which of the underlined words in the paragraph needs to be replaced with its homonym?
   a. led
   b. their
   c. read
   d. wreaked

SUBJECT AND VERB AGREEMENT

A verb must match its subject. If the subject is plural, the verb must be plural, and vice versa.

> The *dogs were* barking.

> The *girl was* late.

Essay Questions

The sets in this final section provide 26 essay-writing topics. These topics are representative of the kinds of writing prompts that you might find on an essay-writing test. As you plan and write practice essays, first choose the topics that are of interest to you or the topics that you know something about. When you begin to feel comfortable writing a 30-minute essay on a familiar subject, try writing about the topics that are less familiar—just to stretch your writing comfort zone.

You will find a scoring guide starting on page 198 of this book, in the Answers section. This guide shows a 6-point scale, with 6 being an excellent essay and 1 being a poor essay. Guides like these are often used by teachers and evaluators of standardized writing tests to score essays. You can use this guide to evaluate your own essays, or you can give the guide and your essay to a friend or teacher for comments. Often, a third party is much better at objectively evaluating your writing than you are.

Also in the Answers section, you will find sample essays for the first six topics in this section (Sets 44–46). These essays will show you how the scoring guide is used to evaluate particular essays.

Generally, you should try for a score of 4 or above on your essays. If your essay falls below a score of 4, revise your work to see if you can raise it to a 5- or a 6-level essay, and show the new version to your evaluator.

SET 44 (Scoring guide on pages 198–199, sample essays start on
        page 199.)

Carefully read the essay-writing topics that follow. Choose one topic on which to write. Then plan and write an essay that addresses all points in the topic that you have chosen.

476. Should public school students be required to wear uniforms? Supporters argue that, among other things, uniforms improve discipline and build a strong sense of community and identity. On the other hand, opponents believe that uniforms limit students' freedom of expression and their development as individuals.

Write an essay in which you take a position on whether or not public school students should be required to wear uniforms to school. Be sure to support your position with logical arguments and specific examples.

477. Recently, American students are said to have fallen behind in the sciences, and some educators believe it is because American teachers are conducting science classes ineffectively.

Write an essay in which you suggest ways that science classes could be conducted so as to more effectively challenge high school and college students.

SET 45 (Scoring guide on pages 198–199, sample essays start on
        page 205.)

Make sure that your essays are well organized and that you support each central argument with concrete examples. Allow about 30 minutes for each essay.

478. Speed limits are part of our everyday lives. Whenever you ride in a car, whether as a driver or passenger, your life is affected by speed limits. Proponents of rigid speed limits claim that lower speed limits save lives, while opponents point out that speed limit laws are unnecessary—and even dangerous.

Write an essay in which you express your opinion about speed limits. Include specific details from your own experiences or observations to support your opinion.

479. Bob Maynard has said that "Problems are opportunities in disguise."
Write an essay describing a time in your life when a problem
became an opportunity. How did you transform the situation?
Explain what you did to turn the problem into an opportunity, and
explain how others can benefit from your experience.

SET 46 (Scoring guide on pages 198–199, sample essays start on
page 209.)
When you write an essay under testing conditions, you should plan on using
about the first one-fourth to one-third of the time you are allotted just for planning. Jot down notes about what you want to say about the topic, and then find
a good way to organize your ideas.

480. In his play, *The Admirable Crighton,* J. M. Barrie wrote, "Courage is
the thing. All goes if courage goes."
Write an essay about a time in your life when you had the courage to do something or to face something difficult, or when you
feel you fell short. What did you learn from the experience?

481. Some people say that writing can't be taught. Educators debate the
subject every day, while the teachers in the trenches keep trying.
Write an essay in which you take a position on this matter. You
may discuss any kind of writing, from basic composition to fiction. Be sure to back up your opinion with concrete examples and
specific details.

SET 47 (Scoring guide on pages 198–199.)
The most important step in writing an essay is to read the topic carefully. Make
sure that you understand the question. If you have a choice of topics, choose
the one you understand fully.

482. Dorothy Fosdick once said, "Fear is a basic emotion, part of our
native equipment, and like all normal emotions has a positive function to perform. Comforting formulas for getting rid of anxiety
may be just the wrong thing. Books about *peace of mind* can be bad
medicine. To be afraid when one should be afraid is good sense."
Write an essay in which you express your agreement or disagreement with Fosdick's assertion. Support your opinion with
specific examples.

483. In the past several years, many state governments have permitted gambling by actually sponsoring lotteries to increase state revenues and keep taxes down. Proponents of gambling praise the huge revenues that gambling generates. Opponents counter that gambling hurts those who can least afford it, and increased availability of gamblers leads to an increase in the number of gamblers who need treatment.

Write an essay in which you take a position on the issue of state-sponsored gambling. Be sure to support your view with logical arguments and specific examples.

SET 48 (Scoring guide on pages 198–199.)
Take just 30 minutes to plan and write your essay. This is good practice for writing under timed conditions, as you have to do in a test.

484. The Western view of human rights promotes individual rights. The Eastern view argues that the good of the whole country or people is more important than the rights of individuals.

Write an essay in which you take a position on this debate. The Western view would be that individuals always have the right to express their opinions. The Eastern view would hold that individual expression must sometimes be fettered in order to promote harmony in a given society. Be sure to support your discussion with specific examples and logical arguments.

485. Barbara Tuchman once noted, "Every successful revolution puts on in time the robe of the tyrant it has deposed."

Write an essay in which you either agree or disagree with her observation. Support your opinion with specific examples.

SET 49 (Scoring guide on pages 198–199.)
When planning your essay, use an outline, a brainstorming list, a topic map, or any other method that works for you to jot down your ideas and organize them logically.

486. Gossip is fun, but if it is malicious, it can be hurtful.

Have you ever been the victim of gossip? Have you ever passed on gossip that you later found was untrue? How do you think the victim of malicious gossip should react or respond? What advice would you give to such a victim?

487. In 1997, scientists in Scotland successfully cloned a sheep. This event added to the debate over human cloning. Proponents of a ban on human cloning are concerned about issues such as genetic selection. Opponents of a ban point out that cloning could lead to significant medical advances.

    Write an essay in which you take a position on the issue of human cloning. Be sure to support your view with logical arguments and specific examples.

SET 50 (Scoring guide on pages 198–199.)
When you write, make sure that the first paragraph of your essay includes a thesis statement, or a sentence that states the main idea of your essay.

488. Law enforcement agencies use a tool called *profiling* in certain situations. Profiling is the practice of outlining the looks and behavior of the type of person who is more likely than others to commit a particular crime. For example, if a person buys an airline ticket with cash, travels with no luggage, and returns the same day, that person fits the profile for a drug courier. Opponents of profiling argue that it has the potential to unfairly target citizens based on their appearance. Proponents argue that law enforcement must take such shortcuts in order to effectively fight crime.

    Write an essay in which you take a position on this debate. Be sure to use logical reasoning, and be sure to support your view with specific examples.

489. Is it ever okay to lie? Some people say that "little white lies" are acceptable to spare someone else's feelings. Other people believe that it is never right to lie, and that telling a few little lies leads to telling more and bigger lies.

    Which position do you hold? Is it possible to never lie? Is it possible to tell just the right amount of lies? Use examples to illustrate your position.

SET 51 (Scoring guide on pages 198–199.)
There is no specific number of paragraphs that you have to have in an essay, but it would be difficult to write a good essay on any topic in fewer than three paragraphs. Most good essays will have four to seven paragraphs.

490. The United States owes the United Nations several million dollars in back-dues and other fees. Opponents of paying this debt point to an inefficient bureaucracy at the United Nations and the tendency of the United Nations to support positions that are not in the United States' best interests. Proponents of paying this debt highlight a growing tendency toward internationalism and the fact that the United States depends on the United Nations for support.

Write an essay outlining why the United States should pay its United Nations debt or why it should not. Support your position with examples and logical arguments.

491. As juvenile crime increases, so do the calls for stricter punishments for juvenile offenders. One suggestion is to lower the age at which a juvenile may be tried as an adult. Supporters of this view believe that young people are committing crimes at younger and younger ages, and the crimes they are committing are becoming more and more heinous. Opponents of this view point to the success of juvenile crime prevention programs, such as teen centers and midnight basketball.

Write an essay in which you either defend or criticize the suggestion that juvenile offenders should be charged as adults at younger ages. Include examples and logical reasoning to support your position.

SET 52 (Scoring guide on pages 198–199.)
The essays in this set and the next few contain more personal topics—ones that ask you to reflect on a specific event in your life or on your personality.

492. Phyliss Bottome has said, "There are two ways of meeting difficulties. You alter the difficulties or you alter yourself to meet them."

Write about a time in which you attempted to alter a difficult situation, or decided to alter yourself. Were you successful? Are you pleased with the choice you made? Whichever you chose to alter, would it have been easier to alter the other? Would it have been better?

493. Bella Lewitzky once said, "To move freely you must be deeply rooted."

Write an essay in which you first state what you interpret this statement to mean (there is no right or wrong interpretation), then (using your own interpretation) agree or disagree with it. Support your opinion with specific examples and logical reasoning.

SET 53 (Scoring guide on pages 198–199.)
Each body paragraph of your essay should have a topic sentence that forecasts the main idea of that paragraph. Make sure that your topic sentences are connected to your thesis statement in order to write a unified essay.

494. Most people have faced a situation—perhaps in a class, an organization, or just with a group of friends—in which they held a strong but unpopular opinion.

Write about a time when you were in this circumstance. Did you speak up? Did you keep quiet? Why do you think you made the choice you did?

495. Do you consider yourself adventurous, a risk-taker?

Write about a time in which you contemplated an undertaking that others considered dangerous. Did you do it? Why? If you did not do it, why not? Do you have regrets? The danger involved need not have been physical, although it could have been.

SET 54 (Scoring guide on pages 198–199.)
It's always important to explain yourself fully. How will the reader understand the event you're describing if you don't "show all"? In both personal and persuasive writing, it's important to include lots of details, images, and explanations to support your main idea.

496. Nadine Stair said, "If I had my life to live over again, I'd dare to make more mistakes next time."

Write an essay in which you agree or disagree with this assessment, using your own life as a touchstone. Why do you agree or disagree? How might your life have been different if you had dared to make more mistakes?

497. In the 1960s and 1970s, women were demanding the right to attend previously all-male educational institutions. Having won that right, some women are now reconsidering. Citing studies that indicate that girls perform better in all-girl schools than in coed schools, some women are calling for the establishment of single-sex educational institutions.

Write an essay in which you take a position on the issue of single-sex schools. Be sure to include specific examples and solid reasoning in your opinion.

SET 55 (Scoring guide on pages 198–199.)
Often, the best way to organize a personal essay is chronologically, in time order. But you should still make sure you have a thesis statement that responds to the question, and that your whole essay is related to your thesis statement.

498. Susanne Curchod Necker said, "Worship your heroes from afar; contact withers them."

Do you agree? Write about a time when you made contact with a hero. Were you disappointed with the experience or not? Or perhaps someone once thought of you as a hero. Did they feel the same way after they got close to you? Did closeness make the relationship better or worse?

499. Most of us have been in a situation, perhaps at work or at school, in which we felt that we were being treated unfairly.

Write about a time when you were treated unfairly. How did you react? What did you do or say about the treatment? If you had it to do over again, would you do something differently?

SET 56 (Scoring guide on pages 198–199.)
Whether you're writing a personal essay or a persuasive one, make sure you stick to the topic you are given.

500. An old cliché says, "You can't fight city hall."

Do you believe this is true? What advice would you give to someone who wanted to convince a city council that a stoplight should be installed at a particular corner? Perhaps you can write about a time in which you tried to change or enact a law, or perhaps a regulation at school or work. Were you successful? Why or why not?

501. Advances in genetic testing now allow scientists to identify people whose genetic backgrounds put them at greater risk for certain diseases. A genetic predisposition to a certain disease, however, does not guarantee that a patient will contract that disease. Environmental factors, such as diet, exercise, and smoking also play a role. Insurance companies want to have access to genetic information in order to help keep their costs down. Opponents feel that insurance companies will misuse such information by unfairly denying people coverage.

Write an essay in which you take a position on providing genetic testing information to insurance companies. Be sure to support your argument with specific examples and logical reasoning.

Answers

Section 1: Mechanics

SET 1 (Page 4)
1. **a.** The first word of a sentence is always capitalized.
2. **b.** Nationalities and languages require capitals.
3. **a.** *Jr.* is a kind of title and therefore takes a capital.
4. **b.** The first letter of a direct quotation takes a capital.
5. **e.** Capitalization is correct.
6. **a.** All words in the proper name of a place require capitals.
7. **b.** Proper names require capitals.
8. **c.** Movie titles are capitalized.

SET 2 (Page 6)
9. **d.** There should be quotation marks before the word *Coach* to set off the dialogue.
10. **d.** Commas set off nonrestrictive appositives, phrases that say the same thing as the previous phrase, in different words. (A comma should be placed after *Patricia*.)
11. **a.** A colon can go before a list. (Place a colon after the word *flowers*.)
12. **c.** Quotations that are questions need a question mark inside the quotation marks.

13. c. A dash can be used to set off a parenthetical element, for emphasis. (Place another dash after the word *senior*.)

14. a. The possessive *Kim's* requires an apostrophe.

15. e. This sentence is punctuated correctly.

16. b. Commas set off parenthetical elements and always go inside the quotation marks in a line of dialogue. (Place a comma after the word *remember*.)

17. d. Commas set off a word or phrase that describes the subject but does not alter the meaning of the entire sentence. (Place a comma after the word *Larkin*.)

18. c. A semicolon can be used to separate two main clauses, which could each stand alone as complete sentences. (Place the semicolon after the word *treadmill*.)

SET 3 (Page 8)

19. b. The comma separates the main clause from the long, descriptive subordinate clause.

20. d. The semicolon can be used to separate two main clauses, which could each stand alone as complete sentences.

21. a. The quotation is a question, and the tag *asked Timothy* ends the sentence.

22. e. The sentence is punctuated correctly.

23. b. The word *student's* is possessive and needs an apostrophe.

24. e. The sentence does not require any punctuation other than the period at the end.

25. c. This is a declarative sentence; it asks an indirect question, so a question mark should not be used. Also, the comma is unnecessary.

26. e. The sentence is punctuated correctly.

27. a. The phrase *as captain of the team* is a nonessential element in the sentence and needs to be set off with commas.

28. d. Commas separate dates and locations.

SET 4 (Page 10)

29. a. *Winter* should not be capitalized.

30. c. There should not be an apostrophe after the word *girls*.

31. a. The comma is unnecessary and should be deleted.

32. b. *Mayor* should be capitalized because it refers to a particular mayor.

33. c. *South Dakota* is a proper noun, and both words should be capitalized.

34. a. This is a declarative sentence; the question mark should be replaced with a period.

35. b. The sentence is a question, so it should end with a question mark.

36. a. The word *state* is not being used as a proper noun, so it should not be capitalized.

37. b. *Lets* is being used as a contraction for "let us," so it needs an apostrophe—*Let's.*

38. a. The words *seeing Betty* form a dependent clause and need commas before and after: *Bill, seeing Betty, walked the other way.*

39. c. The commas are missing from this series of adjectives.

40. b. The quotation mark should appear on the outside of the exclamation point: *"Don't run!"*

41. c. *Polio* and *smallpox* should not be capitalized. Diseases are not capitalized unless a proper noun is part of the name.

42. a. *Ocean* should be capitalized.

43. c. To set off the dialogue, there should be quotation marks before the word *I'll.*

44. c. *Mayor* should not be capitalized because it does not refer to a particular mayor.

45. b. A semicolon is not used between a dependent and an independent clause. Use a comma.

46. b. *Veterinarian* is not a proper noun and should not be capitalized.

47. c. The word *Why*, which begins the quotation, should be capitalized.

48. b. *World War* is a proper noun and should be capitalized.

49. a. The phrase *like many other viruses* should be set off by commas because it is a nonessential element in the sentence.

50. a. *Industrial Revolution* should be capitalized.

51. a. The commas in this sentence should be deleted. Commas are not used in a series when the series is already linked by conjunctions.

52. a. The names of centuries are not capitalized.

53. c. This sentence asks a question and should end with a question mark.

SET 5 (Page 14)

54. c. The second half of the sentence is a dependent clause—it cannot stand on its own as a complete sentence—so it is preceded by a comma.

55. **e.** A quoted question ends with a question mark.

56. **a.** This sentence contains two independent clauses, which are separated by a semicolon. Note that it could be split into two compete sentences.

57. **b.** This sentence also contains two independent clauses. It could be split into two separate sentences, or a semicolon might be used. But the second half explains or defines the first half, so a dash can also be used.

58. **c.** Titles require capitals.

59. **d.** First word of salutations, titles, and proper names all take capitals; a colon follows the salutation in a business letter.

60. **d.** Commas set off parenthetical elements.

61. **a.** A comma goes before *and* when *and* links two main clauses.

Section 2: Sentence Structure

SET 6 (Page 20)

62. **d.** The semicolon after *reunion* indicates that the sentence is made up of two independent clauses. Choices **a** through **c** would be preceded by a comma, not a semicolon.

63. **a.** *Therefore* best completes the sentence's meaning; it creates a cause and effect relationship between how Lila is feeling (the cause) and her decision to stay home from work (the effect).

64. **b.** This sentence establishes a contrast between Dave's past fishing trips and the present one. The best choice, therefore, is *but*.

65. **c.** The sentence requires a condition—Ruby likes blueberry pie on one condition: freshly picked blueberries. Choice **b** can be ruled out because blueberry pie is not always made with freshly picked blueberries. Choices **a** and **d** result in unclear sentences.

66. **a.** *However* indicates an impending contradiction; it is the best choice because the two clauses compare musical tastes. In this case, the comparison contrasts Mitchell's preference to Greg's.

67. **d.** This sentence shows a cause and effect relationship. We want the windows closed *since* (or *because*) we have the heat on.

68. **b.** The two clauses make a reference to time—more specifically, to two different times. Choice **b** is the only logical response.

69. **d.** The golden retriever is never outside without a leash because the neighbor is afraid of dogs; one is the effect of the other.

Consequently means *following as an effect* or *as a result.* This is the best choice.

70. a. This sentence speculates that quilts were made *from* fabrics taken *from* somewhere. Only *from* completes this idea.

71. d. This is the only choice that results in a complete and logical sentence. Choice **a** is illogical; choices **b** and **c** result in sentence fragments.

72. d. The conditional tense, *would have heard,* is the only one that logically fits with the second clause of the sentence.

73. c. The Beatles songs specifically named were pulled from a pool of titles. Only *Among* suggests the existence of many other things, in this case songs.

SET 7 (Page 23)

74. c. *Even though* is the most logical subordinating phrase, showing a contrast. The other choices are not only illogical but ungrammatical.

75. b. In this choice, the subordinate clause makes sense. Choice **b** is also the least wordy of the choices. In choices **a** and **d**, the subordinators are illogical. Choice **c** contains a misplaced modifier (Plato *believed*; Plato's idea could not *believe*).

76. a. The word *despite* establishes a logical connection between the main and subordinate clauses. *Whereupon* and *so that* (choices **b** and **c**) make no sense. Choice **d** is both illogical and ungrammatical.

77. c. The subordinator *because* in choice **c** establishes the logical causal relationship between subordinate and main clause; choices **a** and **b** do not make sense. Choice **d** has faulty construction.

78. b. *Whereas* (in choice **b**) is the logical subordinator, establishing contrast. The other answer choices make no sense.

79. b. There is no cause and effect relationship in this sentence, so choices **a** and **c** do not make sense. Choice **d** begins the sentence with a dependent phrase. Only choice **b** is grammatically correct and logical.

80. c. The two sentences suggest an unexpected contrast: I still don't understand, even though he spoke at length. The best conjunctions to express this would be *yet* or *but.*

81. b. The subordinator *so* (choice **b**) establishes the correct causal relationship between main and subordinate clause. The other subordinators do not point to cause.

82. d. These two sentences suggest a cause and effect relationship: I bought a new car *because* my old one died. Notice that choice **c** is not correct because it begins with a dependent clause.

83. a. The subordinator *whereas* (choice **a**) correctly establishes a contrast between subordinate and main clause. The other choices point to an illogical causal relationship.

84. c. Choice **a** contains a misplaced modifier. Choice **b** is a run-on sentence. Choice **d** establishes a faulty causal relationship between main and subordinate clauses. Choice **c** correctly states a simple fact.

SET 8 (Page 27)

85. c. The conjunction *but* sets the reader up for a contrast or opposite: *TV passive . . .* (but) *computer game active.*

86. b. The conjunction *so* indicates a causal relationship: *Socrates taught* [something obviously controversial], *. . . so he was . . . both loved and . . . hated.* Choice **c** is incorrect because it has a misplaced modifier.

87. a. The conjunction *for* in this sentence means *because* and prepares the reader for a logical causal relationship. Choice **d** is a run-on sentence.

88. a. The conjunction *so* indicates that there is a causal relationship between the two main clauses.

89. d. The conjunction *yet* prepares the reader for a contrast: *respected, yet . . . imprisoned.* Choice **b** is wrong because it is unclear.

90. c. These two sentences express a cause and effect relationship, even though the speaker doesn't know what caused another person's anger. This relationship is expressed by *because.*

91. c. The conjunction *so* indicates a logical causal relationship between the first main clause and the second: *loaded with money, (so) she can afford.*

92. b. The conjunction *but* sets the reader up for an opposite or contrast: *it is possible . . . (but) unlikely.* Choices **c** and **d** make no sense.

93. c. The speaker is asking someone to do two things: come on Thursday *and* bring ice.

94. a. The subordinating conjunction *although* signals an impending contradiction; it makes the most sense. The other choices do not make sense.

95. d. The subordinator *but* contrasts the main clause and subordinate clause in a logical way. Choices **a, b,** and **c** do not make sense.

96. d. The conjunction *although* joins the two sentences by contrasting one with the other. Note that **c** is very similar to **d**, but it begins the sentence with a dependent clause.

SET 9 (Page 30)

97. d. The word *yet* suggests that a condition—*I have no blue shirts*—is contrary to one's expectations. One would expect the speaker to own blue shirts if blue is his favorite color.

98. b. Most of the choices suggest cause and effect; Polly is conceited because she is bright. Only choice **b** provides the needed contrast; she is bright, *but* she is also conceited.

99. c. The word *so* suggests a logical relationship. It is logical that tomorrow will be Saturday if yesterday was Thursday. Notice that choice **d** makes the same logical connection, but it begins with a conjunction (*since*). Remember that conjunctions are used to join two parts of a sentence, and therefore should not be used at the beginning of a sentence where there are not two parts to join together.

100. c. The conjunctive adverb *therefore* establishes the causal relationship between the number of babies in the neighborhood and the neighborhood's nickname.

101. a. The transitional word *however* correctly establishes a contrast between the large number of stores in the shopping mall and the absence of a pet shop.

102. a. The transitional word *furthermore* correctly indicates the addition of one negative trait to another. Choice **d** is incorrect because not everyone who is unreliable has a difficult personality.

103. a. The conjunction *but* means *on the contrary*, and indicates that the two negatives in the first main clause will be followed by their opposite or opposites in the second: *Never eat candy or ice cream . . . (but) do drink soda.*

104. c. The conjunction *but* indicates that the first main clause will be followed by something that indicates an opposite or contrast: is definitely unpleasant . . . *(but)* is not as unpleasant as.

105. d. The conjunction *so* correctly indicates the causality: The subject of the sentence always has a big party because she loves celebrating her birthday. Choice **a** indicates causality but is ungrammatical.

106. b. The conjunction *yet* prepares the reader for a contrast: *is not usually . . . (yet) it can.* Choice **c** is unclear.

107. d. The conjunction *and* in this sentence indicates *also*. Choice **a** is wrong because it is a sentence fragment. Choice **b** makes no sense; choice **c** prepares the reader for a contrast but fails to deliver: *narcolepsy is* occurs in both main clauses.

108. b. The conjunction *yet* prepares the reader for a contrast: *much interest throughout the ages . . . (yet) scientific study . . . is . . . new.* Choices **a** and **c** are incomplete sentences.

SET 10 (Page 33)

109. a. Correct as is. This sentence requires the same form (parallelism) between the verbs *welcome* and *have*, and choice **a** is the only sentence that does this (*welcoming* and *having*).

110. c. All the choices begin with dependent clauses except choice **c**.

111. b. The word *however* functions as a conjunctive adverb in this sentence. Conjunctive adverbs should be preceded by a semicolon and followed by a comma.

112. a. Correct as is. This is the only choice that does not have a faulty subordination. The first part of the sentence is an independent clause; the second part is a dependent clause. Choice **a** is correct because the dependent clause is correctly introduced by the relative pronoun *which*.

113. e. This is the only choice that does not contain repetition or wordiness. In choices **a**, **c**, and **d**, *well known, prominent, famous,* and *renown* mean the same thing; in choice **b**, a painter obviously lived and painted.

114. c. This sentence consists of two independent clauses, each of which could stand on its own as a complete sentence. The two clauses should be separated by a semicolon.

115. a. Correct as is.

116. d. The phrase *growling fiercely* is a nonessential clause, since the sentence would still be complete without it. It should be set off by commas.

117. d. The comparison in this sentence between the United States and Japan requires *as well as*. Choice **d** does this while at the same time creating a clear and logical sentence.

118. a. Correct as is. A comma is needed before a coordinating conjunction and after a subordinating clause; choice **a** is the only one that does both.

119. d. In this complex sentence, choice **d** is the only choice that results in a complete sentence. The other choices are sentence fragments.

SET 11 (Page 36)

120. b. This is the only choice in which the sentence construction is clear and unambiguous. In choices **a** and **c**, the sentence reads as though the ingredients were making the torte. In choice **e**, no one is making the torte. Choice **d** is incorrect because there is a shift in tense from present (*making*) to past perfect (*should have used*).

121. a. Correct as is. The phrase *rather than the rear* is a nonessential clause, and is preceded and followed by commas.

122. e. This is the only choice that does not contain excessive wordiness or a redundancy. In choice **a**, the phrase *the fifth of five* is redundant. Choices **b**, **c**, and **d** also repeats *five* and *fifth*.

123. e. *Roughing It* is the title of Twain's book, and should be set off by commas before and after.

124. d. Choice **d** is correctly punctuated with a semicolon between two independent clauses, and there is no shift in person. Choices **a**, **b**, and **e** are incorrect because the sentence shifts from the first person (*We*) to the second person (*you*). Choice **c** uses a semicolon when no punctuation is necessary.

125. b. In this sentence *contrary to*, which means a viewpoint that is opposite to or in conflict with another viewpoint, is used correctly. In choice **a**, *in* is inappropriately used with opposite. Similarly, choices **c**, **d**, and **e** do not use standard phrasing.

126. a. Correct as is. Choices **b** and **e** are wordy while choices **c** and **d** are awkward.

127. c. Choices **a**, **b**, and **e** are awkward and wordy. Choice **d** is unclear and ambiguous; the use of the preposition *to* distorts the meaning of the sentence.

128. d. This choice is clear, logical, and unambiguous and does not use extraneous words. Choice **a** is redundant: *until the time when*. Choice **b** is also redundant (*since when*) and uses extraneous words. The redundancy in choice **c** is *to kill and stop*. In choice **e**, the phrase *up to when* is awkward, and the word *its* has an unclear referent.

129. a. When constructing sentences, unnecessary shifts in verb tenses should be avoided. Choice **a** is best because all three verbs in the sentence indicate that the action occurred in the past (*had been covering*, *became*, and *was called*). In choice **b**, there is a shift to the present (*becomes*). Choice **c** begins in the present (*is covering*, *becomes*), then shifts to the past (*called*). Choice **d** makes two tense shifts, and choice **e** shifts once, from present to past tense.

130. d. This is the only choice that is both grammatically and logically correct. Choice **a** has a shift in construction; there are two subjects that mean the same thing (*Donald Trump* and *he*). Choice **b** has a modifier problem; the sentence implies that Donald Trump built a billion-dollar empire because he was the son of a real estate developer. Choice **c**, though constructed differently, results in the same faulty logic. Choice **e** creates faulty subordination.

131. e. The correct punctuation between two independent clauses is a semicolon. Choice **a** is wrong because it creates a comma splice. Choice **c** creates a sentence fragment. Choices **b** and **d** create faulty subordination.

132. b. The original sentence begins with a dependent clause, and only choice **b** corrects that error.

133. e. This is the correct choice because the sentence is complete, logical, and unambiguous.

134. b. This is the only choice that is logical and unambiguous.

SET 12 (Page 40)

135. c. This is a sentence fragment.

136. a. The semicolon should be a comma.

137. d. There are no errors.

138. b. This is a run-on sentence.

139. c. The modifier *last summer* is misplaced. A modifier should be nearest to the subject or action that it modifies; in this case, that action is *visited*, not *grew up*. The sentence should read: *Last summer, we visited the town where my father grew up.*

140. d. There are no errors.

141. c. The word *unless* does not logically connect the independent clauses. The sentence needs a word that indicates contrast, because what Liam loves and what Liam can expect are two opposite things; the coordinating conjunction *but* should replace *unless*.

142. a. This is a run-on sentence.

143. b. This is a sentence fragment.

144. d. There are no errors.

145. d. There are no errors.

146. b. The word *that* is unnecessary; two independent clauses use a comma and a coordinating conjunction.

SET 13 (Page 42)

147. a. The other choices are unclear because they are awkwardly constructed, obscuring who intends to set the fire.

148. a. Choices **b** and **c** are sentence fragments. Choice **d** represents confused sentence structure as well as lack of agreement between subject and verb.

149. c. The other choices contain unnecessary shifts in person: from *people* to *their* and *we* in choice **a**, to *your* and *one* in choice **b**, and to *our* and *they* in choice **d**.

150. a. This is the most clear and concise wording, and it avoids beginning the sentence with a dependent clause.

151. b. This is the most clear and concise wording, and it avoids beginning the sentence with a dependent clause.

152. c. This is the only choice that is clear and logical. Choice **a** reads as though the eyes are in the third or fourth grade. Choices **b** and **d** are unclear.

153. c. Choice **c** creates a clear comparison. It is the only choice that is clear and logical.

Section 3: Agreement

SET 14 (Page 48)

154. a. The verb is formed incorrectly; *must of missed* should be replaced by *must have missed*.

155. b. This is an error in subject-verb agreement. The subject, *committed citizens*, is plural and requires a plural verb form. In this case, the correct form is *exceed*, not the singular form, *exceeds*.

156. b. The error is grammatical; there is no subject-verb agreement in this sentence. The subject *Each* is singular and requires a singular verb form. In this situation, the correct form is *has had*.

157. a. This is an error in agreement. The singular noun *one* requires the singular verb *is*. When the subject (in this case *one*) follows the verb, as in a sentence beginning with *here* or *there*, be careful to determine the subject. In this sentence, the subject is not the plural noun *keys*.

158. d. The group *students* is plural, but the subject of the sentence is *one* specific student, so the pronoun should also be singular (*his*).

159. d. In this sentence, there is faulty parallelism. The word *asking* should be replaced by the verb *asked*. This sentence is in the past tense, so the two verbs *asked* and *phoned* should be parallel.

160. d. The subject (*the child*) is singular, so the plural pronoun *their* is incorrect.

161. b. There is no subject-verb agreement in this sentence. The singular collective noun *staff* requires a singular verb form. Therefore, the plural form *deserve* should be replaced with the singular *deserves*.

162. d. This sentence lacks parallel construction. Diana learned *to do* three things: swim, water ski, and hike. The word *to* should be omitted in the portion represented by choice **d.**

163. d. There is no subject-verb agreement in the sentence. The subject of the second independent clause is *filter*, a singular noun. Therefore, the singular form of the verb should be used. The verb *reduce* should be replaced by the verb *reduces*.

164. b. This sentence has a problem with subject-verb agreement. The two subjects of the sentence, *chief executive officer* and *chairman of the board*, require a plural verb. In this case, the singular form *agrees* should be replaced by the plural form *agree*.

165. b. The error is in verb formation. The sentence requires the past tense of the verb *begin*. To correct this error, the past participle *begun* should be replaced with the past tense *began*.

SET 15 (Page 50)

166. c. The sentence requires a verb in the past tense.

167. d. The sentence requires a verb in the past tense.

168. d. The appropriate tense for this verb is the present tense.

169. b. The verbal form *been eating* fits with the verb *have*.

170. c. The imperfect form of the verb *to repair* is needed in this sentence. Imperfect verbs are "uncompleted" or on-going, and frequently end in *-ing*.

171. a. This command is referring to the present, so it requires a verb in the present tense.

172. d. This verb actually refers to something in the past, even though the sentence begins with a reference to the present.

173. c. This sentence refers to something in the future.

174. b. This is the only choice that is in agreement with the singular subject *woman*.

175. c. The correct verb form is the past tense *swung*.

176. b. The verb *are* agrees with the plural noun *restaurants*.

177. a. The singular verb *gets* agrees with the singular noun *noise*.

SET 16 (Page 52)

178. d. A plural subject takes a plural verb; since the subject *words* is plural, the verb *to be carved* must also be plural.

179. a. A *family* is a group of people, but in this sentence they are all acting as one unified whole—everyone in the family shares the same heritage from Nova Scotia. Therefore, the singular verb *is* is correct.

180. d. The three underlined phrases form a list, and each item in the list refers back to the verb phrase *is responsible for*. One would not say, "He is responsible for must evaluate taxes," or "He is responsible for generate revenue." By treating each item individually, the correct answer becomes evident.

181. b. Both *good eyesight* and *more energy* refer back to the verb phrase *gives people*. Only choice **b** maintains that relationship between the verb phrase and the objects (*good eyesight* and *more energy*).

182. c. Only choice **c** puts both verbs in the same tense.

183. d. Choice **d** is best because it is written in the active voice.

184. e. Choice **a** is ambiguous: Is everyone submitting to the council? Choices **b**, **c**, and **d** make an illogical shift in verb tense.

185. b. The second clause of this sentence requires a parallel construction. Choice **b** is the only one in which all four elements use the same grammatical construction, a verb in the present tense followed by a noun.

186. b. This is the best answer because there are no shifts in verb tense. For the sentence to be logical, all the verbs should remain in the past tense.

187. d. *To ensure* means to make certain; *to assure* means to cause a feeling of certainty. The Senator wants his constituents to feel secure; he is not actually securing the money by putting it in a vault. Choice **e** is redundant; the verbs *to assure* and *to promise* mean the same thing.

188. e. Conscience is a moral awareness; conscious is a physical awareness. Josh was awake and physically aware of his environment.
Choices **a** and **b** use the wrong word to describe Josh's condition. In choice **d**, it seems the operation was given a local
anesthetic, not Josh.

SET 17 (Page 54)

189. b. The correct verb form is *applauded.*

190. b. There is no subject-verb agreement. The verb should be plural
because the subject, *plants,* is plural.

191. b. The word *it's* is a contraction of *it is.* It should have been *its,*
which is possessive.

192. c. This is a sentence fragment.

193. b. Saying "should of" instead of "should have" is a common
mistake. The correct tense of the verb is *should have read.*

194. a. The word *holiday* is not capitalized unless it is part of a proper
noun.

195. b. There is no subject-verb agreement. The verb should be plural
because the subject, *photographs,* is plural.

196. d. There are no errors.

197. b. The correct verb form is *has broken.*

198. a. The correct verb form is *rang.*

199. b. The sentence makes an illogical shift in tense—from the past to
the present tense.

200. b. There is no subject-verb agreement. The verb should be
singular because the subject, *one* (not *boys*), is singular.

201. c. The correct verb form is *has worn.*

202. a. This sentence makes an illogical shift in tense—from the past to
the present tense.

SET 18 (Page 56)

203. a. The verbs *got* and *took* agree in tense.

204. d. The verbs *liked* and *got* agree in tense.

205. a. *Became* and *eating* are the correct forms of the verbs.

206. a. This is a complete sentence; the others are fragments.

207. d. This is a complete sentence; the others are fragments.

208. b. This is a complete sentence; **c** and **d** are fragments; in choice **a**
the verb does not agree in number with its subject, *one.*

209. b. This is a complete sentence; the others are fragments.

210. a. Only choice **a** is both logical and a complete sentence.

211. a. This sentence demonstrates a common source of confusion. The easiest way to make sense of it is to remove *Mike and* from each choice. For example, *Please go to the movies with I* is clearly not correct, so choice **a** is best.

212. d. In this sentence, the verb tense between the independent clause and the subordinating clause agree. In choice **a**, the lack of agreement in tense makes the sentence unclear as to time; choice **b** doesn't make it clear who ate the popcorn; choice **c** implies that the popcorn watched the movie.

SET 19 (Page 58)

213. e. There are no grammatical, idiomatic, logical, or structural errors in this sentence; choice **e** is the best answer.

214. a. *Their* should be replaced with the contraction *They're*, meaning *They are*.

215. d. This is a grammatical error. The contraction *it's* (meaning *it is*) should be replaced by the possessive pronoun *its*.

216. e. There are no grammatical errors in this sentence; the best answer is choice **e**.

217. e. There are no grammatical errors in this sentence; choice **e** is the best answer.

218. a. This sentence begins with a dependent clause, signaled by the word *because*. Sentences should not begin with conjunctions, as a general rule.

219. c. The word *each* is singular, not plural. Therefore, the plural pronoun *their* is incorrect.

220. e. There are no grammatical errors in this sentence; choice **e** is the best answer.

221. d. The word *there* should be replaced by the possessive pronoun *their*.

222. c. The pronoun *me* should be replaced by the pronoun *I*. In this sentence, *my brother*, *my Aunt Clarissa*, and *I* is the subject, and the nominative (subject) case is required. *Me* should be only used as an object pronoun.

223. e. There are no grammatical errors in this sentence; choice **e** is the best answer.

224. a. This sentence has an agreement problem. The plural pronoun *them* does not agree with the singular noun *glossary*. Therefore, *them* should be replaced by the singular pronoun *it*.

225. b. *Your* should be replaced by *you're*. Because these two words are pronounced alike, they are often confused. *Your* indicates possession and *you're* is the contraction of *you are*.

226. e. There are no grammatical, idiomatic, logical, or structural errors in this sentence; choice **e** is the best answer.

227. e. There are no grammatical, idiomatic, logical, or structural errors in this sentence; choice **e** is the best answer.

SET 20 (Page 60)

228. b. The correct form of the pronoun is *me* (objective case).

229. c. The correct pronoun is *who*, because it refers to a person, and it is the subject form of *who* (not the object form, *whom*), because *who* is doing something, making candied figs.

230. b. The pronoun agrees in number with the noun to which it refers.

231. b. The antecedent, *George and Michael*, is plural, so the plural pronoun *their* is the correct choice.

232. c. The pronoun *that* agrees in number with the noun to which it refers, *hat*.

233. c. The pronoun *them* agrees with the plural noun *flowers*.

234. d. *She and I* is the subject of the sentence, so the subjective case is needed.

235. a. The possessive case is used before the word *taking*, because it functions like a noun in this sentence.

SET 21 (Page 61)

236. b. There are two potential problems in this sentence: 1) the grammatical agreement between the nouns *Kendra or Zoë* and the pronoun *her*; and 2) the formation of the verb *to bring*. In choice **b** both of these are correct. Because the sentence reads *Kendra <u>or</u> Zoë*, the pronoun must be singular; only one of them brought the volleyball. *Brought* is the past tense of *bring*. Choice **a** is wrong because the pronoun *their* is plural. Choice **c** is wrong because *there* is not a correct pronoun. Choices **d** and **e** are incorrect because *brang* is not the past tense of *bring*.

237. a. This choice is the only one that uses the proper form of possessive pronouns.

238. c. *Person* is singular, but *their* is plural. The correct answer, choice **c**, is singular.

239. e. This is the only choice that displays agreement between the subject and verb and between the pronoun and its antecedent.

240. d. When the relationship between a pronoun and its antecedent is unclear, as it is in this sentence, it should be changed to avoid ambiguity. There are two boys, Andre and Robert, and choice **d** makes the relationship clear: Robert's family moved, and not Andre's family.

SET 22 (Page 63)

241. c. The word *I* should be replaced with the word *me*, because the pronoun is the object, not the subject.

242. d. There are no errors.

243. d. There are no errors.

244. c. The correct pronoun is *I*, not *me*.

245. b. The contraction *who's* is incorrect. The correct usage is the possessive *whose*.

246. b. This sentence contains a shift in number. *Bears* is a plural noun, so the clause should read: *they were growling*.

247. d. There are no errors.

248. c. The contraction *Three's*, which means *Three is*, is the correct usage.

249. a. The correct usage is the possessive *theirs*, not *there's*.

250. a. *Either* is incorrect. Use *either* with *or* and *neither* with *nor*.

251. a. The pronoun *him* is incorrect. *He* should be used because *you* and *he* are the subjects of the dependent clause.

252. b. The contraction *You're* should be replaced with the possessive *Your*.

253. c. This sentence makes a shift in person. It should read: *The committee members should work as hard as they can.*

254. d. There are no errors.

255. d. There are no errors.

SET 23 (Page 65)

256. b. Choice **a** is similar, but it begins with a dependent clause. The other choices are not logical.

257. d. These sentences show cause and effect, but only choice **d** makes logical sense.

258. b. This is the only choice that is clear and unambiguous. All the other choices contain misplaced modifiers, resulting in unclear and illogical statements.

259. c. This is the only choice that is grammatically correct. Choices **a** and **d** use the verbs incorrectly. Choice **b** uses *a* instead of *an* before anthology.

Section 4: Modifiers

SET 24 (Page 69)

260. b. In this sentence, *loud* modifies the verb *screamed*. The adverb *loudly* should be used instead of *loud*.

261. e. There are no errors in this sentence; choice **e** is the correct answer.

262. d. This sentence makes a comparison between Frieda and three other girls; therefore, the superlative *tallest* should be used. *Taller*, the comparative form, is incorrect because it compares only two people.

263. e. There are no errors in this sentence; choice **e** is the best answer.

264. e. There are no errors in this sentence; choice **e** is the best answer.

265. d. The double comparative *more cozier* is redundant; just the comparative word *cozier* is sufficient to convey the idea that New York movie theaters will become more comfortable with the addition of love seats.

266. e. There are no errors in this sentence; choice **e** is the best answer.

267. a. The boy was describing his state of health, or well-being, so the adjective *well* should be used rather than *good*.

268. d. This sentence makes a comparison between many house guests. Therefore, the superlative word *most* should be used. *More* only compares two things.

269. c. In this sentence, *hesitant* attempts to modify the verb *walked*. The adverb *hesitantly* should be used instead of *hesitant*.

270. a. Use *bad* when modifying a noun; use *badly* when modifying a verb. The verb *treated* should be modified by the adverb *badly*, not the adjective *bad*.

SET 25 (Page 71)

271. a. The missing phrase modifies the verb *are armed* and creates a comparison between two types of people, heroes and villains. Therefore, you need a comparative form of the adverb *heavily*.

272. c. The comparison is between two things, a cake made last week and a cake made this week; choices **a** and **d** can be ruled out. Choice **b**, *more better*, is redundant. Choice **c**, *better*, is the best choice to make the comparison.

273. d. The missing phrase modifies the verb; therefore the sentence requires an adverb. Choices **a** and **b** are adjectives and can be ruled out. Choice **c** makes an unnecessary comparison.

274. b. The comparison is being made among three brothers; therefore, this sentence requires a superlative. Choices **a** and **c** only compare two things, and choice **d** is redundant.

275. a. The missing phrase modifies a noun and makes a comparison between two things, what he thought and what it was; therefore the sentence requires a comparative adjective. Choice **b** is an adverb. Choice **c** does not make a comparison, and choice **d** is a superlative, a comparison of three or more things. Choice **a**, *more terrifying*, is the best choice.

276. d. Use *fewer* with nouns that can be counted.

SET 26 (Page 72)

277. d. Adjectives modify nouns and adverbs modify verbs. In choice **d**, the adjectives *frightening* and *unhappy* correctly modify the noun *ending*. In choices **a** and **b**, the adverb *frighteningly* incorrectly attempts to modify a noun. In choice **c**, the adverb—*unhappily*—incorrectly attempts to modify a noun. Choice **e** is unnecessarily wordy.

278. b. The sentence makes a comparison between Adela and all other members of the graduating class; therefore, the superlative form *most* should be used. Choices **a** and **d** are wrong because they use the comparative *more*. Choice **c** is wrong because the word *importantly* is an adverb and cannot modify the noun *member*. Choice **e** is wrong because it uses the word *like* incorrectly.

279. a. The word *than* is a conjunction used to indicate a comparison, and used as a conjunction, it is followed by the the pronoun *I*. The word *conservatively* is an adverb modifying the verb *dresses*. Choice **a** is the only one that correctly makes the comparison and uses the adverb correctly.

280. e. This is the correct choice because the sentence does not contain a double negative. The other choices either use two negative words within a single sentence or use an incorrect comparative form of easy.

281. **a.** The sentence compares an individual and an entire crowd of individuals; therefore, it requires a superlative. Only choice **a** coherently uses the superlative *happiest* to make the comparison among all the many people in the crowd.

282. **d.** When a comparison is made, the word *fewer* is used with nouns that can be counted; the word *less* is used with quantities that cannot be counted.

283. **d.** This sentence makes a comparison between strip mining and all other types of mining; therefore, it requires a superlative. Choices **a** and **b** compare only two things while choice **e** inappropriately uses an adverb. Choice **c** uses a double superlative and is redundant.

SET 27 (Page 73)

284. **d.** There are no errors.

285. **a.** The adjective *sad* should be replaced with the adverb *sadly*, which correctly modifies the verb *wandered*.

286. **a.** This sentence contains a double negative.

287. **d.** There are no errors.

288. **d.** There are no errors.

289. **a.** This sentence has a usage error: *fewer mistakes*, not *less mistakes*.

290. **d.** There are no errors.

291. **a.** *Between* is only used to refer to two things. *Among* is the correct word to use in this sentence.

292. **d.** There are no errors.

293. **c.** *Most awfulest* is a double superlative, and therefore redundant.

Section 5: Paragraph Development

SET 28 (Page 78)

294. **a.** This is the best choice because it is the only one that refers to recycling containers, which is the main focus of this paragraph. The other choices are statements about recycling in general.

295. **b.** This is the only choice that mentions telecommuting, which is the main focus of this paragraph. The other choices are too general.

296. **c.** This choice refers to "unreasonable searches," which is the main focus of this paragraph. Choice **a** can be ruled out because this idea is not developed by the other two sentences. Choices **b** and **d** do not relate to the topic of unreasonable searches.

297. b. This choice clearly fits with the main focus of the paragraph, which is the skill that is needed to hand-rear orphaned baby birds. Choice **a** is too vague to be a topic sentence. Choices **c** and **d** introduce other topics.

298. c. The main focus of the paragraph is the height of a wave. This is the only choice that introduces that topic.

299. a. The paragraph expresses the writer's opinion about respect for the law. Choices **b** and **d** can be ruled out because they are irrelevant to the main topic. Choice **c** can also be eliminated because it discusses respect for other people, not respect for the law.

300. b. Choice **b** addresses both of Gary's vanities: his person and his situation. Choice **a** deals only with Gary's vanity of person. Choice **c** deals only with his vanity of position. Choice **d** is not supported in the passage.

301. d. The use of phrases like *changed the course of history* and *nations have actually gone to war* implies that the subject of the paragraph is history; these phrases also connote danger and intrigue.

302. a. This sentence introduces the topic of painting models and miniatures. The other sentences provide supporting ideas, but not the main topic.

303. b. Each sentence may be true, but only choice **b** introduces the specific farm that the paragraph discusses. The paragraph is about Wheeler Farm, not about Silas Wheeler.

304. b. The paragraph addresses the dangerous nature of power mowers, and only choice **b** introduces that topic.

305. a. The paragraph addresses changes in the company's vacation policy, and choice **a** introduces that topic. Choices **b** and **c** are addressed in the paragraph, but neither refers to the overall topic.

306. d. This choice specifically defines the kind of hearsay evidence that is admissible in a trial and would be logically followed by a definition of the kind of hearsay evidence that is inadmissible. It works better as a topic sentence than choice **c**, which is more general. Choices **a** and **b** contradict the rest of the paragraph.

307. c. Choice **c** is the only choice that prepares the reader for the fact that the paragraph constitutes a set of instructions for workers.

308. d. Choice **d** is the only sentence that focuses on both the tickler system and its usefulness to secretaries, and therefore is relevant to all the other sentences in the paragraph. Choices **a** and **b** are too general to effectively focus the paragraph; choice **c** is too narrow.

309. c. This choice focuses most sharply on the main topic of the paragraph—muscle atrophy and bone loss. Choices **a** and **b** are too broad to guide the reader to the focus of the paragraph. Choice **d** is too limited.

310. a. The word *rather* indicates a contrast to whatever came before. Choice **a** is the only sentence that guides the reader to the contrast between the old definition of asthma and the new. Choices **b** and **c** are less precisely related to the new understanding of asthma. Choice **d** is not related at all.

311. a. Choice **a** is more specific than the other choices and more sharply focused toward the entire paragraph. Choices **b** and **d** are more vague and general, and choice **c** is written in a slightly different, more upbeat style.

SET 29 (Page 85)

312. a. Choice **a** expands on the topic sentence. Choices **b** and **c** do not relate directly to indoor pollution. The style of choice **d** is more informal than that of the topic sentence.

313. c. This choice directly illustrates the topic sentence. Choice **a** does not mention the Middle Ages, choice **b** does not mention red hair, and choice **d** is unrelated to the topic sentence.

314. a. The topic of this paragraph is weed killer, not weeds; nor is proper care addressed.

315. c. The idea expressed in the topic sentence is counterintuitive, as stated in choice **c**. (The words *This idea* also gives an important clue, since an idea is the subject of the topic sentence.) The other choices do not relate directly to the nature of light.

316. b. The topic is Internet communication, not computers. Choice **c** does address communication, but not as it relates to the Internet.

317. c. Choice **c** expands on the list of good reasons to eat organic food. The other choices are simply neutral facts.

318. d. Choice **d** helps explode the myth spoken of in the topic sentence by giving alternatives to student loans. The other choices do not deal directly with the idea expressed in the topic sentence.

319. b. The topic sentence is obviously from a contract and speaks of an agreement. Choice **b** goes on to explain, in the language of a contract, what that agreement is and so is more closely related to the topic sentence than the other choices.

320. d. This is the only choice that logically follows the topic: It provides a possible reason why Americans are fascinated with reality television. The other choices do not follow the topic sentence.

321. d. Only this choice addresses something mentioned in the topic sentence: the fact that pasta is easy to prepare. The other choices address topics not mentioned in the first sentence.

322. a. This is clearly the only choice that logically follows the statement about juries in colonial times. Choices **b** and **c** can be ruled out because they do not refer back to colonial times. Choice **d** refers to colonial times but not to juries.

323. c. This choice develops the topic sentence by providing information about what a landscaper would recommend under these conditions. Choices **a**, **b**, and **d** veer away from the topic.

324. b. This is the only choice that develops the topic sentence. Choice **a** does not even mention gingko. Choice **c** is redundant because Europe is part of the world. Choice **d**, by referring to an old study, veers completely away from the topic.

325. a. Only this choice addresses something mentioned in the topic sentence: the fact that cats have good hygiene. The other choices address topics not mentioned in the first sentence.

SET 30 (Page 89)

326. d. The passage is about the cassowary bird, not about human beings. Sentence 4 is irrelevant to the topic.

327. c. The passage is about the nature of storytelling and has nothing to do with writing programs.

328. b. The passage has to do with Caribbean cuisine. People traveling to the Caribbean for vacation is irrelevant to the main topic.

329. c. The focus of the paragraph is ratatouille, not zucchini.

330. c. This is the only sentence that does not mention sleepwalking, which is the subject of the passage.

331. d. Although there is a connection between Lyme disease and deer ticks, this connection is not made in the paragraph.

332. d. The first three sentences are written in an objective, professional tone. The tone of Sentence 4 is much more personal and subjective so even though it says something about a harp, it is quite out of character in this paragraph.

333. b. This is the only sentence that mentions religion or any human activity at all. The other sentences define the solstices in lay science terms.

334. a. The other three sentences objectively discuss the role and qualifications of a meteorologist. Sentence 1 tells us what people think of weather forecasters. Its tone is also much more casual than the rest of the paragraph.

335. b. This choice has the objective tone of a textbook and is a general statement. The other choices describe a particular child and are written in a fictional style.

336. b. Choices **a**, **c**, and **d** list specific characteristics of the two different types of ghosts, benevolent (good) and malevolent (bad). Choice **b** is just an ironic observation on the general subject of ghosts.

337. d. The first three sentences address different types of weight-lifting exercises, while the fourth sentence addresses the topic of trainers at local gyms.

338. b. The topic of this paragraph is the writings of C. S. Lewis, not his life story. Where he lived is not specifically related to the types of books that he wrote.

339. a. Choice **a** addresses different sizes and shapes of ladders, while the rest of the paragraph deals with the dangers of ladders being placed near power lines.

340. c. The paragraph as a whole discusses the various parts of a book, but Sentence 3 addresses the topic of bookstores.

341. c. This choice is a general statement about CO poisoning. The other choices all relate to a firefighter's specific duties in dealing with victims of CO poisoning.

SET 31 (Page 95)

342. d. This is the correct order of the events described in the paragraph.

343. c. Sentence 2 gives an overview of what the paragraph is about. Sentence 3 gives specific reasons why Sentence 2 is correct. Sentence 1 gives the reason why Sentence 3 is correct.

344. **b.** Sentence 1 provides a statement about adding a treat to a child's lunchbox periodically and gives no indication, by its tone or its wording, that it is based upon any other sentence. Sentence 4 tells us that in spite of the truth in that statement, it is best, as a general rule, to provide healthy snacks and it uses the word *however*, which indicates that it is responding to another idea which we've already heard. Sentence 2 with the word *usually*, gives a definition of what is considered a healthy snack. Sentence 3 goes on to provide specific examples of healthy snacks.

345. **b.** Sentence 3 is the topic sentence and states the main goal of the neighborhood association. Sentence 2 goes on to cite specific tasks that help the association achieve that goal. Sentence 1, with the word *Additionally*, tells us that there is one more thing the association does, even though it is a less frequent and less primary responsibility.

346. **a.** In this choice, the order is chronological. In Sentence 4, they take Grandma to the Greyhound station. In Sentence 2, the bus has not yet moved away from the station. In Sentence 1, the bus jolts away but is still in town. In Sentence 3, the bus (at least in the narrator's mind) is out on the open highway.

347. **a.** Sentence 1 is the topic sentence. Sentence 4 defines the term *double jeopardy* used in Sentence 1; Sentence 2 gives another definition, signaled by *also*; Sentence 3 begins with the word *Finally* and gives the last definition.

348. **c.** Sentence 3 is clearly the lead sentence as it tells us something about the new employee handbook and is in no way based on information provided in the other two sentences. Sentence 2 uses the word *also* to indicate that it is telling us something else about the handbook, something that adds to a fact we've already been told. Sentence 1, which is making a generalization about the new policies, is based on information we already know from Sentences 3 and 2. Because of this, it can only follow these sentences and not precede them.

349. **a.** Sentence 2 sets the stage—this is a memory. After that, the order is chronological: In Sentence 1, the man tries to teach his son how to pitch. In Sentence 4, he wasn't interested, so he gave up. Sentence 3 logically follows—the memory of giving up makes him feel sad and guilty.

350. d. Sentence 4 sets the reader up to expect a discussion of a procedure. Sentence 3 tells how you can find the right report forms. Sentence 1 leads logically into Sentence 2.

351. a. Sentence 2 is the topic sentence. Sentence 1 provides reasons for the procedure described in the topic sentence. Sentence 3 gives further definition as a conclusion.

352. d. The word *Yet* at the beginning of Sentence 1 is a clue that this is not the beginning sentence. Sentences 4 and 1 are the only ones that logically follow each other, so the other choices can be ruled out.

353. c. Sentence 1 introduces the topic of carburetors. Sentence 2 defines what a carburetor is, while Sentence 4 explains its importance. Sentence 3 provides a conclusion to the paragraph.

354. b. Sentence 2 is the topic sentence, introducing the subject. Sentence 3 expands the topic, and Sentence 1 concludes with a general observation on the use of irises.

355. a. Sentence 1 introduces the topic, while Sentence 2 develops it. Sentence 3 draws a conclusion from the first two sentences.

SET 32 (Page 99)

356. b. Paragraph 2 contradicts the misconceptions potential adopters of racing greyhounds might have about the breed. Choice **b** states that certain popular beliefs about greyhounds are erroneous and acts as a transition to the facts that follow in the paragraph. Choice **a** does not focus on contradicting the misinformation; also, the phrase *even so* appears to agree with the misconceptions rather than contradict them. Choice **c** does not focus on the argument; instead, it repeats information given in the previous sentence. Choice **d**, rather than supporting the main purpose of the paragraph—which is to dispel myths about racing greyhounds—actually contradicts information in Parts 6 and 7.

357. b. The possessive pronoun *their* is correct.

358. c. This choice is the best because it retains the writer's informal, reassuring tone and because the information in it furthers the purpose of this paragraph—i.e., the suitability of greyhounds as household pets. This response also is clearly directed at a general audience of householders. Choice **a** is incorrect because the information does not keep with the topic of the paragraph; also, the tone set by the inclusion of a precise statistic is too formal. Choice **b** retains the informal tone of the selection but it provides information already given in the first paragraph and not suitable to the purpose of this paragraph. The tone in choice **d** is argumentative, which defeats the author's purpose of trying to reassure the reader.

359. c. This question tests the ability to recognize a sentence fragment. Although choice **c** does include a subject and a verb, it is a dependent clause because it begins with the adverb *when*. Choices **a**, **b**, and **d** are all standard sentences.

360. a. This question assesses the ability to recognize redundancy in a sentence. Choice **a** removes the redundancy of Part 8 by taking out the word *also*, which repeats the meaning of the introductory phrase *in addition to*. Choices **b** and **c** involve changing singular nouns to plural and plural possessive nouns, which is not necessary and would make the sentence grammatically incorrect. Choice **d** would change the meaning of the sentence incorrectly. The attitude of the community toward young people is being reported, not what young people have reported about the community attitude.

361. c. Choice **c** provides a fact that supports and expands upon the information given in the previous sentences. The first two sentences tell us about the program's success and the plans for expanding it. The third sentence builds upon these ideas by providing detailed information about the results of the program and who was involved. Choice **a** changes the subject of this paragraph. This paragraph is about the program in a specific school district and choice **a** makes a comment about other school districts, which may be true, but which is not related to the topic of this particular paragraph. Choice **b** adds a detail about the program but it is a single detail as opposed to a conclusive, summarizing sentence that gives us a clear idea of the program specifics. Choice **d**, which mentions the possibility of other pilot programs, again, changes the subject and veers away from the main topic of this paragraph which is the Mural Painting Program within this particular school district.

362. d. This question tests the ability to recognize standard sentence structure. Part 2 is an incorrectly punctuated compound sentence—a comma splice. Choice **d** correctly joins the two simple sentences into a compound one by using a semicolon in place of the comma. Choice **a** creates an error in subject-verb agreement. Choice **b** is incorrect because a dash cannot join two simple sentences into a compound one. Choice **c** turns the first phrase of the sentence, *Deciding on the hamburger steak special,* into a dangling modifier.

363. b. This question assesses the ability to recognize the correct use of modifiers. The phrase *After tasting each of the dishes on my plate* is a dangling modifier; the sentence does not have a subject pronoun this phrase could modify. Choice **b** is correct because it supplies the missing subject pronoun *I.* Choices **a**, **c**, and **d** are incorrect because they let the modification error stand; none of them provide a subject pronoun the phrase could modify.

SET 33 (Page 103)

364. b. This question assesses the ability to recognize the correct agreement of subject and verb. Choice **b** is correct because it uses the third-person singular of the verb to be, *is,* which agrees in number and in person with the subject *one.* Choice **a** is wrong because it does not correct the subject-verb agreement problem; instead, it removes an optional comma between *location* and *and.* Choice **c** is incorrect because it does not correct the agreement error, instead, it makes an unnecessary change in vocabulary from *increase* to *enhance.* Choice **d** is incorrect because it does not correct the agreement problem; instead, it creates an error by misplacing the modifier *only* directly after the semicolon.

365. d. This question tests the ability to recognize the logical connection of ideas in a paragraph and to recognize grammatical consistency. Choice **d** gives a general piece of advice (start walking), which is followed by two sentences that point to things that will result from following this advice. Choice **a** is incorrect because although it does give a general piece of advice that would make sense at the beginning of this paragraph, it contains an error in the pronoun/antecedent agreement (using the pronoun *people,* which disagrees in person with the antecedent *you*). Choice **b** is incorrect because it includes other forms of physical activity (jogging, bicycling) that are off the topic (walking) and are irrelevant to the development and order of ideas in the passage. Choice **c** is incorrect because it contains the same pronoun/antecedent agreement problem as choice **a**, and the sentence does not respect the order of ideas in the paragraph; it returns, in the third paragraph of the passage, to information and ideas that are more appropriate to the first paragraph.

366. a. Choice **a** is correct because a comma after the word *rewards* in Part 3 closes off the parenthetical phrase between the subject, *physical activity*, and the predicate, *will*. Choice **b** is incorrect because it introduces an incomplete comparison into Part 1. Choice **c** is incorrect because it adds an unnecessary comma into Part 5. Choice **d** is incorrect because it adds a misplaced colon to Part 2.

367. b. The word *appraised*, meaning *judged*, does not make sense in the context; the correct word for the context is *apprised*, meaning *informed*. Choices **a, c,** and **d** are all incorrect because the words *incriminate, criteria,* and *ascertain* are all used correctly in context.

368. c. The information in Part 5 continues the description of what judges must ascertain about such cases, which began in Part 3. Skipping next to the responsibilities of officers and back to judges, as happens in the passage as it stands, is confusing. Choices **a** and **b** are incorrect because they introduce examples before the passage states what the examples are supposed to show. Choice **d** is incorrect because deleting Part 2 removes the statement from which all the paragraph's examples and information follow.

369. c. Part 4 contains a run-on sentence; the conjunction *however* requires the use of either a colon or semicolon before it in order to link two sentences. The other choices are incorrect because the parts they indicate contain standard sentences.

370. d. This choice provides the plural reflexive pronoun *themselves*, which agrees in number and person with the subject, *Those*. Choice **a** is incorrect because it provides the verb *combine* which does not agree in person or in number with the subject, *snowboarding*. Choice **b** is incorrect because it removes a hyphen necessary to the creation of compound adjectives. Choice **c** is incorrect because it changes the verb to the past tense, which does not agree with the present tense used throughout the paragraph.

371. b. The topic of the passage is Abraham Lincoln's effectiveness as a leader. The fact that his picture is on U.S. currency is irrelevant.

372. c. The word *nation* is not being used as a proper noun and does not need to be capitalized. The other choices do not need to be changed; they are grammatically correct as is.

373. b. Part 5 contains the comparative form *more*, but the sentence only includes one side of the comparison. The phrase *someone . . . may feel more tired* is an incomplete comparison because it does not state what people feel more tired than. Choices **a**, **c**, and **d** are incorrect because these parts do not contain incomplete or faulty comparisons.

374. a. This question requires the ability to infer the logical relationships between ideas in a sequence. In this case, relationships are, first, between stated fact and the conclusion or hypothesis drawn from the fact (*since*); and, second, between the hypothesis and a particular illustration supporting the hypothesis (*For example*).

SET 34 (Page 108)

375. d. This question calls on the ability to identify standard usage of the possessive. Choice **d** is correct because the word *researchers* is actually a possessive noun, and so an apostrophe must be added. Choices **a** and **c** are incorrect because they substitute misused homonyms for the words given. Choice **b** is incorrect because it contains a faulty pronoun/antecedent—the *microprobes* have a diminutive width, not the brain.

376. b. In Part 4, the adverb *typically* is misused as an adjective to modify the noun wire. The other choices do not contain nonstandard uses of modifiers.

377. c. The phrases *since they [microprobes] are slightly thinner than a human hair* and *because of their [microprobes'] diminutive width* contain the same information.

378. b. The predicate does not match the subject grammatically, which is necessary when using the verb *is*: *A passenger-created disturbance* doesn't match *by playing . . . or creating.*

379. c. This choice makes use of parallel structure because the list of the conductors' obligations are all expressed in the same subject/verb grammatical form: *Conductors will wait, will allow, will not allow.* In choices **a**, **b**, and **d**, the parallelism of the list is thrown off by the last item in the list, which changes the subject of its verb from operators to passengers.

380. b. Part 6 contains a nonstandard use of a preposition. The standard idiom is *comply with* rather than *comply to*. Choices **a, c,** and **d** do not contain nonstandard uses of prepositions.

381. b. Part 6 contains a sentence fragment; the sentence is a dependent clause. Choices **a, c,** and **d** all refer to standard sentences.

382. c. The main purpose of this paragraph is strictly informational, to outline Dr. Miranda Woodhouse's plan to reduce the risks of heart disease, and choice **c** focuses the reader's attention on the four strategies that Dr. Woodhouse proposes as part of this plan. Choice **a** contains seemingly contradictory information which is in no way implied or stated in the paragraph. Choice **b** focuses on the life expectancy rates of American citizens and while lowering heart disease may boost life expectancy rates, this paragraph does not deal with that at all. It focuses exclusively on Dr. Woodhouse's plan for preventing heart disease. Choice **d** makes an argumentative claim about one part of Dr. Woodhouse's plan, which is out of place in a paragraph that seeks only to outline the basic strategies.

383. c. The possessive pronoun *their* is used erroneously in Part 9. *There* is the word that should be used.

384. c. A comma is necessary after the first part of the sentence, which is an introductory phrase. Choice **a** is incorrect because visiting London, Paris, and Rome was not dependent on her being ten years old, so the word *Because* doesn't make sense. Choice **b** is incorrect because a comma after *Although* is unnecessary and makes the sentence grammatically incorrect. Choice **d** is incorrect because the word *breathtaking* is describing a noun (*scenes*) and requires an adjective, not an adverb. *Breathtakingly* is an adverb.

385. b. Part 2 contains a sentence fragment. Choices **a, c,** and **d** are incorrect because they all contain standard sentences.

386. c. The semicolon in Part 6 must be followed by an independent clause, and here it is followed by a dependent clause. Choices **a, b,** and **d** are incorrect because they all contain standard sentences.

387. b. The underlined word in Part 7 needs to be made into a plural noun. Choice **a** is incorrect because it is a singular noun which makes for incorrect subject-verb agreement. Choices **c** and **d** are incorrect because they are possessive.

SET 35 (Page 113)

388. b. End quotation marks must be inserted before the tag phrase, *says Warner*. Choice **a** is incorrect because the quotation marks are necessary to begin the quotation again after the tag phrase. Choice **c** is incorrect because *the beverage case* is not a clause that should be set off with commas. It is essential to the meaning of the sentence. Choice **d** is incorrect because *than* is a conjunction used to compare things and is the word that should be used here.

389. b. *Memorize* does not really make sense in this context. A more appropriate word might be *mimic* or *imitate*. Choices **a**, **c**, and **d** are word choices that all make sense within the context of this paragraph.

390. d. Part 5 acts as a topic sentence for the ideas and quotations in the third paragraph. Combining Part 5 with paragraph 3 makes the subject of the third paragraph clearer to the reader and brings information on the main topic together in the same place. Choice **a** would not really make any major difference in the paragraph and doesn't do anything to help focus attention on the main idea. Choice **b** would make the main idea less, not more, clear. Choice **c** would just make for a much longer sentence without adding any emphasis to the main idea.

391. c. The first paragraph mentions that saving room for herbs such as lavender, sage, thyme, and parsley is a characteristic of a thrifty gardener, but fails to explain why it is a sign of thrift. Choice **a** is incorrect because it removes information that is vital to explaining why the plants mentioned in Part 1 are appropriate to a gardener who has little time. Choice **b** is incorrect because reversing the order of the sentences moves the demonstrative pronoun *these* in Part 2 too far away from its antecedent. Choice **d** is incorrect because the passage does not indicate that growing roses is easy in general; rather, it suggests particular types of roses (hardy species) as appropriate to a garden that requires little time for maintenance.

392. a. This sentence creates a transition between the idea of harvesting food from a garden and the proper way of planting in order to achieve a good yield of food. Choice **b** is incorrect because it is redundant, repeating information already stated in Part 5. Choice **c** contains information that is on the subject matter of the first paragraph and is, thus, off-topic in the second. Choice

d is off-topic and does not match the main idea of the paragraph; it mentions time-consuming work in a paragraph on the subject of gardening that takes a moderate amount of time.

393. b. The word *lavished* should be substituted for *languished* because it makes no sense in the context.

394. c. Part 4 contains a nonstandard verb form, *brung*, as the past-tense form of *to bring*; the correct verb *is brought*. Choices **a**, **b**, and **d** are incorrect because they do not contain nonstandard usages of verbs.

395. b. Part 3 contains a sentence fragment, for there is no main verb in the sentence. Choices **a, c,** and **d** are incorrect because they are complete sentences.

SET 36 (Page 116)

396. b. Part 3 requires a comma before the coordinate conjunction *so*. Choice **d** is incorrect because it already shows a comma separating the two independent clauses. Choices **a** and **c** are incorrect because each contains only one independent clause.

397. a. This answer is in the simple past tense, which is the tense used throughout the paragraph. Choices **b, c,** and **d** are incorrect because they suggest tenses inconsistent with the tense of the rest of the paragraph.

398. b. The context requires that the noun *renown* be replaced by the adjective *renowned*. Choice **a** is incorrect because the change to *when* makes no sense in the context; it would imply that Augustus grew up before immigrating. Choice **c** incorrectly inserts the contraction of subject and verb *it is* in a context where the possessive pronoun *its* is required. Choice **d** is incorrect because it introduces a diction error into the sentence.

399. b. The semicolon in Part 2 is used incorrectly to introduce a list. In choices **a, c,** and **d**, the semicolon correctly separates two independent clauses.

400. c. The expressions *year-round* and *in all seasons* repeat the same idea. Choices **a, b,** and **d** are incorrect because none of these sentences contain unnecessary repetition. Part 4 may seem to, at first; however, the words *hot* and *humid* are described in more interesting and specific terms in the second part of the sentence.

401. b. The subject of Part 3 is climate and therefore requires the third-person singular form of the verb to be—*is*. Choice **c** is incorrect because the comma is correctly placed after an introductory phrase. Choice **a** incorrectly inserts the possessive pronoun *its* in a context where the contraction of subject and verb *it is* is required. Choice **d** is incorrect because the comma is necessary to close off the interruptive phrase, *whether in the back country or at established campgrounds*, between the subject and verb.

402. c. Part 7 provides information about the high cost of healthcare insurance. It doesn't give information about the main topic of this passage, which is how to choose a doctor. Choices **a**, **b**, and **d** are incorrect because all of these sentences provide information about, and guidelines for, choosing a doctor.

403. a. An adverb is required here because the word is being used to add information to a verb (*responds*). The correct form of the word is *quickly*. Choice **b** is incorrect because the term *more better* is grammatically incorrect. Choice **c** is incorrect because in the context of this sentence, using the past tense, *accepted*, is not appropriate. Choice **d** is incorrect because the sentence requires an adjective here, not an adverb.

404. a. In Part 1, the adjective *good* is misused as an adverb; it needs to be replaced by the adverb *well*.

405. a. In Part 4, the verb *assure*, to make certain, is nonsensical in the context; it should be replaced by the verb *assume*, to suppose or take for granted. Choices **b**, **c**, and **d** are incorrect because all these words are used properly in their context.

406. d. The paragraph consistently uses the pronoun *you*; therefore, the inconsistent use of *our* should be replaced by *your*. Choice **a** is incorrect because the comma is necessary before the coordinate conjunction *but*. Choice **b** is incorrect because insertion of a colon would incorrectly divide a phrase. Choice **c** is incorrect because it would introduce an error of tense shift into the paragraph.

SET 37 (Page 120)

407. a. The word *greek* in Part 2 should be capitalized. Nationalities and languages require capitalization. Choice **b** is incorrect because a person's title, given before his or her name, should be capitalized, while **d** is incorrect because the title should not be capitalized when no name is given. Choice **c** is incorrect because the names of seasons are not capitalized.

408. a. Part 1 contains a run-on sentence. It requires a semicolon after the parentheses and before *we*. Choices **b**, **c**, and **d** are incorrect because the numbered parts they indicate all contain standard sentences.

409. b. The context requires a word meaning to surrender or yield, so choice **b** is correct. The other choices are incorrect because each has the wrong meaning for the context of the sentence.

410. d. To make the pair of verbs in the sentence parallel, *overlooking* should be changed to *overlooks* to match the form of the verb *towers*. Choice **a** is incorrect because the change would convert Part 7 into a run-on sentence. Choice **b** is incorrect because *Irish*, as the name of a people, must be capitalized. Choice **c** is incorrect because the word *running* is functioning as an adjective here; the verb *run* would make nonsense of the sentence.

411. d. A comma is required after an introductory dependent clause. Choice **a** would introduce a comma fault, separating a verb from its object. Choice **b** is incorrect because the semicolon would have to be followed by a complete sentence, which is not the case. Choice **c** is incorrect because removing the colon would create a run-on sentence.

412. c. Choices **a** and **b** would cause an unwarranted shift in tense from past (in which most of the passage is written) to present. Choice **d** would change the correctly written noun, *effect*, to an incorrect verb form. (*Affect* is a verb, except when used as a noun to denote a person's emotional expression, or lack thereof, as in: *He has a joyless affect.*)

413. b. The adjective *shallow* in Part 5 actually modifies the verb *set*; therefore, the adjective should be revised to be the adverb *shallowly*. Choices **a**, **c**, and **d** are incorrect because none of them contain a nonstandard use of a modifier.

414. c. The proper noun *Lake* must be made possessive because it is followed by the gerund *arriving*. Choice **a** is incorrect because it introduces a comma fault into the sentence. Choices **b** and **d** introduce errors in diction into the sentence.

SET 38 (Page 123)

415. c. This paragraph is about how to handle business phone calls. Reversing the order of Parts 9 and 13 would cause the paragraph to follow the natural order of the beginning to the end of a phone conversation. Choice **a** is incorrect because the information in Part 9, though misplaced, is essential information and should not be deleted. Choice **b** is incorrect because both Parts 8 and 13 need to come near the beginning of the paragraph, for they contain information about handling messages. Choice **d** is incorrect because the addition of such a sentence would repeat information already given or implied in the rest of the paragraph.

416. b. This sentence requires the adverb *then* in this context. Choice **a** is incorrect because it would introduce a problem of agreement between the pronoun *they* and its antecedent *pitch*. Choice **c** is incorrect because it would introduce a problem in subject/verb agreement. Choice **d** is incorrect because the possessive rather than the plural of the noun *boss* is necessary in this context.

417. d. The verb *depend* is, idiomatically, followed by the preposition *on*; in Part 10, it is wrongly followed by *in*. Choices **a**, **b**, and **c** are incorrect because none of them contain nonstandard uses of prepositions.

418. a. The antecedent of the pronoun *they* in this sentence is *someone*. Since *someone* is singular, the corrected subject pronoun should be *he* or *she*.

419. c. The sentence requires the contraction *we're*, short for *we are*. It is all right to use a contraction because the writer uses contractions elsewhere in the passage. Choice **a** is incorrect because it introduces an error in modifiers. Choice **b** is incorrect because a semicolon must be followed, here, by a full sentence. Choice **d** is incorrect because the singular *a deadline* would disrupt the parallelism of the list, the other elements of which are plural.

420. a. Choice **a** is the most logical sentence because it continues to develop the subject of the first paragraph: Patrick Henry. The other choices are mentioned, but they are not the main topic.

421. d. Part 5 changes from the past tense to the present tense with the verb *closes*. It should read, "He *closed* that famous speech. . . ."

422. a. Another sentence is needed to add the information that the program is only for passengers leaving the bus, not those boarding it. This information is implied in the paragraph but not directly stated; without the direct statement, the paragraph is confusing, and the reader must read between the lines to get the information. Choice **b** is incorrect because it removes an important instruction to drivers, rather than clarifying the paragraph's point. Choice **c** is incorrect because it adds information that contradicts the point the paragraph is making. Choice **d** is incorrect because it would place intervening material between the ideas of what the program is and how it operates; it would disorder the sequence of ideas.

423. **a.** The subjective pronoun *who* is incorrectly used to refer to the Stop Here Program; the pronoun *which* would be a better choice.

424. **b.** Part 5 contains two sentences linked only by a comma; a semicolon is required. Choices **a**, **c**, and **d** are incorrect because they all contain standard sentences.

425. **d.** In Part 4, a semicolon is used incorrectly to introduce a list; it should be replaced by a colon. Choice **a** is incorrect because this sentence would not make sense if the contraction *we're*, which means *we are*, replaced the verb *were*. Choice **b** is incorrect because it would introduce a comma fault between the subject *others* and the verb *were*. Choice **c** is incorrect because the comma is needed to separate items in a list.

SET 39 (Page 127)

426. **a.** The phrase *figure out* is slang, and could be replaced by *determining*. It also is in the wrong verb tense.

427. **c.** The verb *calls* should be in the past tense, *called*.

428. **a.** The word *Latitude* is not being used as a proper noun and does not need to be capitalized.

429. **a.** The apostrophe should be removed—*employers* should be plural here, not possessive.

430. **b.** A comma should be added after *leak* to separate the clauses.

431. **a.** Choice **a** is written in the tone and style reflected in the passage. Choices **b**, **c**, and **d** are awkward versions of the same details.

432. **d.** The verb needs to be singular to agree with the singular subject of the sentence, *Theodore Roosevelt*. Choices **a**, **b**, and **c** are incorrect because they introduce a shift in tense.

433. **a.** The subject of the second paragraph is the characters in Dickens' novels. The other choices do not introduce that topic.

434. **c.** The sentence repeats itself several times. *Ordinary people facing extraordinary difficulties* is sufficient by itself, while *things that are hard and unusual* and *regular people* are merely redundant.

435. **d.** There is a verb disagreement between *these* (plural) and *is* (singular). The sentence should begin, *This alone is. . . .*

436. b. The word *Carnavale* is a foreign word; therefore, it must be italicized. Choice **c** is incorrect because there is no reason to italicize the word *serfs*, an ordinary noun, in the passage. Choice **a** is incorrect because the definite article is not needed before the word *Carnival* used as a proper noun. Choice **d** is incorrect because the verb *were* is used correctly here, in the subjunctive mood.

437. a. The objective pronoun *her* is misused in Part 1 as a subject pronoun; it needs to be replaced with the pronoun *she*.

438. a. Quotation marks need to be inserted before the quotation is resumed after the interrupting phrase, *the brochure informed her.* Choice **b** is incorrect because the comma is required to set off the interrupting phrase from the quotation. Choice **c** is incorrect because the close quotation marks are necessary before the interrupting phrase. Choice **d** is incorrect because the quotation is not finished; it goes on for another sentence.

439. b. This statement maintains the formal tone established by the rest of the passage. Choices **a, c,** and **d** are still too informal.

440. d. In Part 7, the pronoun *you* needs to be changed to *we* to agree in number and person to the antecedents used earlier in the passage. Choices **a, b,** and **c** are incorrect because none of these sentences contain a nonstandard use of a pronoun.

441. a. *Consequently* means *as a result of.* The adverbs listed in choices **b, c,** and **d** do not address this sequence.

442. c. Choice **c** reflects the sentiments in the last sentence of the passage. Choices **a, b,** and **d** do not state such a profound effect.

443. b. The pronoun *my* needs to be changed to *our* to agree in number and person withthe pronoun *we*. Choices **a, c,** and **d** fail to correct the pronoun/antecedent agreement problem.

444. a. Part 1 is a fragment and needs a verb to make it a complete sentence. The sentences in choices **b, c,** and **d** are complete.

445. b. The main idea of this paragraph is that, while genius has a recognizable pattern, the patterns are extraordinary. Choice **b** directly states that the patterns have the eerie quality of fate. Choice **a** does not focus ideas, but rather repeats material already stated. Choice **c** focuses attention on the side idea of the popular opinions about genius. Choice **d** contains material that is irrelevant to the main idea and argument of the passage.

446. a. The possessive *Mozart's* is required before the gerund *composing*. Choice **b** is incorrect because *too*, meaning excessively, is required in this context, not the preposition *to*. Choice **c** is incorrect because the possessive form does not make sense in this context. Choice **d** is incorrect because *there*, not the possessive pronoun *their*, is required in this context.

447. c. Part 4 contains an error in pronoun/antecedent agreement; the pronoun *they* must be changed to *it* in order to agree in number and person with its antecedent, *regularity*. Choices **a**, **b**, and **d** are incorrect because they contain standard uses of pronouns.

448. d. The passage discusses the fact that the Hornblower books are both educational and enjoyable. The fact that they are available in paperback and hardcover is irrelevant to the passage's topic.

449. c. The phrase *hero's career* is possessive—the career of the hero—and therefore, *heros* needs an apostrophe. The plural of *hero* is *heroes*.

450. c. Sentence 4 shifts from the past tense to the present tense with the verb *is*. The sentence should read, ". . . what life *was* like . . . ."

451. b. There should be a comma after *secret*, since the sentence contains two clauses.

452. d. Sentence 3 needs a comma after *ordinary people*, separating the two clauses.

453. c. *To correctly divide* is a split infinitive. The infinitive is *to divide*. Choices **a**, **b**, and **d** do not make this kind of error.

454. a. The context requires a verb that means *to extend beyond*, not *to come before*. The words in the other choices do not have this meaning.

455. b. Part 2 is the only interrogatory sentence in the passage. Since it asks a question, it needs a question mark as punctuation.

SET 42 (Page 137)

456. a. Since the sentence states that the *system is designed to give*, then it needs *to ensure* as well. Choices **b**, **c**, and **d** are correct as written.

457. c. The pronoun *his* should be replaced with *their* in order to agree with *federal employers*. There are no errors in pronoun agreement in choices **a**, **b**, or **d**.

458. d. A semicolon should separate two complete sentences (independent clauses); the second half of Part 6 is not a complete sentence but a restatement of a portion of the first half. This makes a colon appropriate. Choices **a** and **b** would create run-on sentences. Choice **c** would incorrectly separate two independent clauses joined by a conjunction (*and*) with a semicolon.

459. c. The pronoun is one of the subjects of the sentence, and so it should be changed from the object form *him* to the subject form *he*. Choice **a** is incorrect because *their*, meaning belonging to *them*, is correct in this context. Choice **b** is incorrect because the comma is necessary before the conjunction. Choice **d** is incorrect because the possessive form is not required in this context.

460. d. Part 5 is the only sentence fragment in this passage. It needs a subject in order to express a complete thought.

461. d. The word *recently* is the best contrast to *Finally though* in Part 2. Choices **a**, **b**, and **c** indicate time lapses that would not necessarily take place in the context of the passage.

462. a. The comma is needed to set off the introductory clause from the independent clause. Making the changes stated in choices **b**, **c**, or **d** would create a nonstandard sentence.

463. b. The phrase *at the ceiling* should be replaced with *on the ceiling*.

464. d. The pronoun *it* should be changed to *they* to agree in number and person with its antecedent, *detectors*. Choices **a**, **b**, and **c** are incorrect because they contain standard uses of pronouns.

465. c. The paragraphs are related in that they both talk about the physical effects of extreme heat on people and the treatment of these conditions, but the main subject of each paragraph details a different condition resulting from extreme heat. The second paragraph begins by mentioning that heat stroke is much more serious than the condition mentioned in Paragraph 1, heat exhaustion. Choice **c** best aids the transition by ending the first paragraph with an explanation of the most serious effects of heat exhaustion, thereby paving the way for the contrasting description of the far more serious condition, heat stroke. Choice **a** is off-topic; choices **b** and **d** are both about heat stroke, so they belong in the second paragraph, not the first.

466. b. The main idea of this paragraph is a description of the symptoms and treatment of heat stroke. The information in Part 7 about the most common victims of heat stroke is least relevant to the topic of the paragraph. The other choices, by contrast, all either discuss symptoms or treatment.

467. a. Part 1 is a sentence fragment; it contains no main verb.

SET 43 (Page 142)

468. c. The phrase *what the occupants been doing* needs an auxiliary verb—for example, it might read *what the occupants* <u>had</u> *been doing*. Choices **a**, **b**, and **d** are incorrect because they contain standard verb forms.

469. a. Part 2 contains a comma splice; the comma should be replaced with a semicolon. Choices **b**, **c**, and **d** are incorrect because they contain standard sentences.

470. b. Part 2 expresses two complete thoughts as one. To correct this sentence, a comma should be added after *Greenland* and the conjunction *but* should precede the independent clause.

471. d. Even though it may look like a question, Part 6 is not an interrogatory sentence. It should not be punctuated with a question mark.

472. c. This choice adds the subject *he* in the second sentence, eliminating the dangling modifier *walking down the street*. Otherwise the sentence reads as if the leaves are walking down the street. All other choices ignore the problem of the dangling modifier and add grammatical mistakes to the sentences.

473. b. This paragraph's purpose is descriptive; it describes the classroom and the corridor outside it. Choice **b** is correct because the information in the sentence adds to the description of the corridor. Choice **a** is incorrect because it adds information that describes the course Howard is to teach, which is not the subject of this paragraph. Choice **c** is incorrect because it adds information about the two buildings mentioned in the first paragraph; therefore, it rightfully belongs in the first paragraph, not the second. Choice **d** is incorrect because it adds information irrelevant to the paragraph.

474. c. Part 6 is a dependent clause with no independent clause to attach itself to; therefore, it is a sentence fragment.

475. d. The word *wreaked* should be replaced in this context by its homonym *reeked*. Choices **a**, **b**, and **c** are all incorrect because the words indicated are all used correctly in their context.

Section 6: Essay Questions
Essay Scoring Criteria

Use the following scoring guide to score each of your essays. Better yet, have someone else read your essay and use the scoring guide to help you see how well you have done. Sample essays for the first six essay topics follow this scoring guide.

A **"6" essay** is a highly effective response to the assignment; a few minor errors are allowed. It has the following additional characteristics:

- Good organization and overall coherence
- Clear explanation and illustration of main ideas
- Variety of sentence syntax
- Facility in language usage
- General freedom from mechanical mistakes and errors in word usage and sentence structure

A **"5" essay** shows competence in responding to the assigned topic but may have minor errors. Additionally, it has the following charactersitics:

- Competent organization and general coherence
- Fairly clear explanation and illustration of main ideas
- Some variety of sentence syntax
- Facility in language usage
- General freedom from mechanical errors and errors in word usage and sentence structure

A **"4" essay** displays competence in response to the assignment. It has the following additional characteristics:

- Adequate organization and development
- Explanation and illustration of some key ideas
- Adequate language usage
- Some mechanical errors and mistakes in usage or sentence structure, but such errors are not consistent

A **"3" essay** shows some competence but is plainly flawed. Additionally, it has the following characteristics:

- Inadequate organization or incomplete development
- Inadequate explanation or illustration of main ideas
- A pattern of mechanical mistakes or errors in usage and sentence structure

A **"2" essay** shows limited competence and is severely flawed. Additionally, it has the following characteristics:

- Poor organization and general lack of development
- Little or no supporting detail
- Serious mechanical errors and mistakes in usage, sentence structure, and word choice

A **"1" essay** shows a fundamental lack of writing skill. Additionally, it has the following characteristics:

- Organization that is practically nonexistent and general incoherence
- Severe and widespread writing errors

A **"0" essay** does not address the topic assigned.

SET 44, Sample Essays (Page 148)

476.
Sample "6" Essay
It may seem to contradict the ideal of democracy upon which our public school system is based, but requiring public school students to wear uniforms is a good idea. In fact, uniforms would help schools provide a better education to all students by evening out socioeconomic differences and improving discipline among students.

Style is important, especially to children and teenagers who are busy trying to figure out who they are and what they believe in. But in many schools today, kids are so concerned about what they wear that clothing becomes a major distraction—even an obsession. Many students today are too busy to study because they're working after school so they can afford the latest fashions. If students were required to wear uniforms, they would have less pressure to be "best dressed" and more time to devote to their studies.

More importantly, the competition over who has the hottest clothes can be devastating to the self-esteem of students from lower-income families. Because uniforms would require everyone to wear the same outfits, students from poorer families would not have to attend school in hand-me-downs nor would they face the kind of teasing they often get from students who can afford name brands. True, students from wealthier families may wear nicer shoes and accessories, but in general the uniforms will create an an atmosphere of equality for all students.

Contrary to what opponents argue, uniforms will not create uniformity. Just because students are dressed the same does not mean they won't be able to develop as individuals. In fact, because uniforms enable students to stop worrying so much about their appearance, students can focus more on who they are on the inside and on what they're supposed to be learning in the classroom.

Furthermore, uniforms will improve discipline in the schools. Whenever a group of people dresses alike, they automatically have a sense of community, a sense of common purpose. Uniforms mean something. School uniforms will constantly remind students that they are indeed in school—and they're in school to learn. Getting dressed for school itself will be a form of discipline that students will carry into the classroom.

Though many students will complain, requiring public school students to wear uniforms makes sense. Students will learn more—both about themselves and about the world around them.

Sample "4" Essay

I don't think that requiring public school students to wear uniforms is a good idea. The way the student dresses makes a powerful statement about who he or she is, and the school years are an important time for them to explore their identities. Uniforms would undermine that. They would also have little, if any, positive affect on students with disipline problems.

Each student has their own personality, and one way he expresses who he is is through his clothing. Clothes are an important way for young people to show others how they feel about themselves and what is important to them. If public school students are forced to wear uniforms, this important form of self-expression will be taken away.

I remember back when I was in junior high school. My parents had given me complete freedom to buy my back to school wardrobe. They took me to the mall and let me choose everything, from sweaters and shirts to socks and shoes. I'll never forget how independent that made me feel. I could choose clothing that I liked. I did make a few bad choices, but at least those were my choices. Students today, I am sure, would feel the same way.

Besides, America values individuality. What happens to that value in an environment where everybody looks the same?

Though disipline in schools is a serious concern, uniforms are not the answer. Disipline problems usually come from a lack of disipline at home, and that's a problem that uniforms can't begin to address. A student who is rowdy in the classroom isn't going to change their behavior because they are wearing a white shirt and tie. In fact, disipline problems might increase if students are required to wear uniforms. Students often make trouble because they want attention. Well-behaved students who used to get attention from how they dressed might now become trouble-makers so they can continue to get attention.

Uniforms are not the answer to the problems public school students face. In fact, because they'll restrict individuality and may even increase disiplinary problems, they'll only add to the problem.

Sample "3" Essay

I don't think that requiring public school students to wear uniforms is a good idea. Each student has their own identity and express who he is through clothing. The school years are an important in finding one's personality. Uniforms would also have little, if any, positive affect on students with disipline problems.

In junior high school I let my children buy their back-to-school wardrobe, anything they wanted. I let them choose everything. I'll never forget how that made them feel. As they would say, awesome! They could choose clothing that they liked.

We are told to be yourself. But how can a young person be in a country where everybody is the same.

Disipline in schools is of a serious concern, uniforms are not the answer. It is the home life of many students that make bad behavior. If the parents use drugs or dont disipline children at home, thats a problem that the school and uniforms can't do anything about. A student who is causing trouble at school isn't going to change their behavior because they are wearing a white blouse or pleated skirt. In fact, disipline problems might even get worse if students are required to wear uniforms because of not getting enough attention about the way he or she is dressed.

Uniforms are not the answer to the problems public school students face. In fact, because they will keep them from being who they are they will make it worse.

Sample "1" Essay

Public school students should wear uniforms to. Not just private school students. I do not want to teach in a private school; but I like them wearing a uniform every day. The look neat and well-groom no matter if they are low income or high income. Social level doesnt matter.

Wearing uniforms is good because they build a sense of community. Everyone from the same school wear the same clothes. The students know if someone is from there school right away. It makes it easier for students, rich or poor, to make friends with people. They don't have to worry about what to wear in the morning because they always know.

Also they don't have to spend as much money on cloths.

Many students think it is unfair that public school students could wear whatever they wanted. Maybe private school students shouldn't wear uniforms either. Then everyone would be able to dress the way they want to and be individulistic.

Some people say uniforms would make bad students behave better. Because they wouldn't always be talking about who has a better sneakers or better jeans. They might have paid more attention in school like they should of, and then everyone could learn more.

477.

Sample "6" Essay

The best way for teachers to boost their students' science test scores is to make students excited by science with real-life examples. Before ever asking students to memorize facts, the teacher should demonstrate a scientific process or even teach students how to experiment for themselves. This allows them to understand the process with their senses before trying to fix it in their intellect.

The following examples could be used to provide anticipation of a lesson to come. First, when studying insects, the teacher might pass around an ant farm in the classroom and let students observe the little anthropods going about their complex, individual tasks before asking the student to read that ants have a rigid social structure, just as people do. If possible, it would be even better to take them on a field trip to see how ants build hills outdoors.

Another example is to let students have hands-on experience with telescopes. Close observation of far-away objects is magical; the rings of Saturn really exist! The Sea of Tranquility, a crater on the moon's surface looks as close as a building on the next block. This introduction to the galaxy and the universe brings the opportunity for lessons about the earth's rotation and about the geophysical facts of the craters that comprise the moon's laughing face. Lessons like these come alive in a way that does not exist in lecture format.

This approach to teaching science should not begin in high school or college but in grade school or even in kindergarten. Scientific facts are important, of course, but without them we have no real understanding. Curiosity is as vital to learning as the ability to memorize, perhaps more so. Curiosity will keep students learning long after they've passed their final test in school.

Sample "4" Essay

Science is important for many reasons, but especially because today's world is based on technology. If other countries get ahead of us in science the consequences may be dire. So it is extremely important for our students to excell.

The first and best way to teach science is to make the student see the practical application of it. For example, if the teacher is teaching botony, she might explain the medical uses of plants. Or if teaching physics, she might show a diagram of a rocket ship. Field trips are a good idea, as well, perhaps to a factory that makes dolls. The point is to make it practical and interesting to boys and girls alike.

When I was in high school I had a teacher named Mr. Wiley who let us mix things in jars and watch the results. Sometimes they were unexpected! Such as a kind of mushroom we planted that was poisonous and reminded us of the horror movies we all loved in those days. Mr. Wiley made it interesting in a personal way, so that it wasn't just dry facts. And he told us the practical uses, such as this particular kind of mushroom is used in the making of certain insect poison.

In this day and age it is important for all of us to know something about science because it affects all aspects of our lives, but for young people it is vital. Their livelihoods—and even their lives—may depend on that knowledge.

Sample "3" Essay

Science is a necesary skill because it can effect each one of us, such as the making of the hydrogen bomb or finding a cure for AIDS. It is responsable for TV, cars, and a host of other items we take for granted. So we all depend on it and need to learn it.

The best way to teach science is to have a good textbook and also good equiptment in the classroom. If the equiptment is poor there is no way they are going to learn it, which is why the poorer schools are behind the richer ones and also behind other countries. Its the most important factor in the classroom today.

Another way to teach science is through field trips and vidio-tapes. There are many tapes in the library and every school should have a good vidio system. Also a good library is importent. And there are many places to take the class that they would find intresting.

When I was in school I thought science was boring. I wish I had learned more about it because I think it would make me a better teacher someday as well as better understand the world of technology. If we don't understand technology we are at it's mercy, and it is something we rely on to get us through our lives. Without science we would have no technilogical advances. If other countries are ahead of us it is our own fault for not putting science as a priority.

Sample "1" Essay

Science is importnt and we should teach it to our students in the right way. A scientist coming in to talk would be one way. Also experimints that the students can do. The reason it is important, is other countrys are ahead of us and we may have a war. Then if there tecnoligy is better they will take us over. So it is dangerous not to have students that know alot about science.

If we teach our children to relay too much on science and technoligy what will happen if it fails. If the computers fail we are in serious trouble. Businesses will suffer and medical research will suffer. So science is important and our students should learn but it isnt everything and they should learn that they should study other things to, like how to make a good living for there family.

If we teach science in the right way our country will be better off as well as our children when they are caught up to the new melinnium

Set 45 (Page 148)

478.

Sample "6" Essay

I believe that speed limits are both unnecessary and burdensome, and in some cases they can be positively dangerous. Unnecessary laws should be removed from a community's legal statutes, because they add to a police department's burden of work by calling on the officers to enforce a law that accomplishes nothing.

Furthermore, speed limit laws are burdensome to the general public because they demand that law-abiding citizens pay careful attention to something that simply doesn't matter. After all, it is not a moral issue how fast one moves in a car; a person is not determined to be "good" or "bad" based upon how fast he drives.

Yet speed limit laws actually have that very effect upon society: a person actually is deemed to be "law-abiding" or a "law-breaker" based on whether or not he obeys speed limits! The very law itself artificially creates a new category of criminals, criminals whose only crime has been that they drove their car faster than some traffic committee thought safe.

But the most important reason for abolishing speed limits is that they can be very dangerous. How often have you suddenly found yourself slamming on the brakes because you discovered a hidden *speed trap*? Every year, thousands of motor vehicle accidents are caused by such speed traps, as motorists panic or slow down to *rubber neck* as they drive past. Even the simple act of taking one's eyes off the road to check the speedometer leads to countless life-threatening situations.

Unnecessary laws are bad laws; laws that endanger those who obey them are very bad laws. There is no question about it: speed limit laws should be repealed.

Sample "4" Essay

Speed limit laws are sort of neutral, it seems to me. They are not really either right or wrong in themselves, what makes them right or wrong is how people use them. A person can be a good driver even if he or she goes fast, and someone else might drive slow and still be a bad driver.

Speed limits don't actually make someone a better driver. For example my grandmother drives pretty slow but she can't see very well. One day, a dog ran in front of the car and she didn't see it until it was too late. Driving slow didn't make it so that my grandmother saw the dog any better, but it did keep the dog alive. So in that sense, the law proved neutral—she didn't drive any better, but the dog wasn't killed.

Laws can't make someone better or worse. Laws only control what people do, not how well they do it. Speed limits control how fast a person drives, but they don't make a person a more skillful driver. There are definitely situations where a driver needs to be warned that the road is dangerous and he needs to drive slower. Driving slower will prevent the car from skidding off the road, and that's the role of speed limits.

On the other hand, there are probably lots of places where speed limits don't accomplish much. Near schools, for example, the speed limit is usually much lower, but slowing down near a school doesn't accomplish anything. When speed limits are helpful, they should be kept, and where they're not helpful they should be removed.

Sample "3" Essay

I'm really glad there's speed limits. Especially since my life got saved once. They're very important for society.

When I was 6 I ran into the rode after my ball in front of a car. She skidded and almost hit me but I jumped back to the sidewalk. Now, if she'd been going fast I would of been killed! But fortunately for me, the speed limit there was 25 and she could stop her car and I had time to jump.

Imagine if their were no speed limits at all! People would be zooming all over the place like crazy, and cars would be skidding. Out of control! The roads and highways today are dangerous enough without turning everyone loose to drive like they were on the way to a fire.

No, the speed limits are too important to get rid of them. Like I said, I'm alive because of them!

Sample "1" Essay

If your not careful speeding will kill you I know what I'm talking about because I've seen it happen. Just last week a guy hit the gard rale because he wasn't paying attention. In front of my house.

Laws are good. We need more in fact. If anything I think cops should have better rights to arrest people who won't do the law. Including driving there cars.

But 65 is to slow I think on the highway. Whats the sense of going slow when everyones going the same way. But on backroads there good.

479.

Sample "6" Essay

Life is full of problems, but the method we use to approach those problems often determines whether we're happy or miserable. Bob Maynard says, "Problems are opportunities in disguise." If we approach problems with Maynard's attitude, we can see that problems are really opportunities to learn about others and ourselves. They enable us to live happier and more fulfilling lives.

Maynard's quotation applies to all kinds of problems. To share a personal story, I faced a problem just last week when our family's kitchen sink developed a serious leak. Water puddled all over our new kitchen floor, and to make matters worse, our landlord was out of town for the week. Since my family is large, we couldn't afford to wait for the landlord's return nor could we afford an expensive plumbing bill. Taking charge, I decided to learn how to fix it myself. The best place to start was at my local library. There, I found a great fix-it-yourself book, and in just a few hours, I had figured out the cause of the leak. Not only did I repair the leak, but I know now that I can rely on my own abilities to solve other everyday problems.

I think it's important to remember that no matter how big a problem is; it's still an opportunity. Whatever kind of situation we face, problems give us the chance to learn and grow, both physically and mentally. Problems challenge us and give us the chance to do things we've never done before, to learn things we never knew before. They teach us what we're capable of doing, and often they give us the chance to surprise ourselves.

Sample "4" Essay

Just the word "problem" can send some of us into a panic. But problems can be good things, too. Problems are situations that make us think and force us to be creative and resourceful. They can also teach us things we didn't know before.

For example, I had a problem in school a few years ago when I couldn't understand my math class. I started failing my quizzes and homework assignments. I wasn't sure what to do, so finally I went to the teacher and asked for help. She said she would arrange for me to be tutored by another student who was her best student. In return, though, I'd have to help that student around school. I wasn't sure what she meant by that until I met my tutor. She was handicapped.

My job was to help her carry her books from class to class. I'd never even spoken to someone in a wheelchair before and I was a little scared. But she turned out to be the nicest person I've ever spent time with. She helped me understand everything I need to know for math class and she taught me a lot about what it's like to be handicapped. I learned to appreciate everything that I have, and I also know that people with disabilities are special not because of what they can't do, but because of who they are.

So you see that wonderful things can come out of problems. You just have to remember to look for the positive things and not focus on the negative.

Sample "3" Essay

The word "problem" is a negative word but its just an opportunity as Mr. Bob Maynard has said. It can be teaching tool besides.

For example, I had a problem with my son last year when he wanted a bigger allowance. I said no and he had to earn it. He mowed the lawn and in the fall he raked leaves. In the winter he shovelled the walk. After that he apreciated it more.

Its not the problem but the sollution that matters. My son learning the value of work and earning money. (It taught me the value of money to when I had to give him a bigger allowance!) After that he could get what he wanted at Toys Are Us and not have to beg. Which was better for me too. Sometimes we forget that both children and there parents can learn a lot from problems and we can teach our children the value of over-coming trouble. Which is as important as keeping them out of trouble. As well we can teach them the value of money. That is one aspect of a problem that we many times forget.

So problems are a good teaching tool as well as a good way to let you're children learn, to look at the silver lining behind every cloud.

Sample "1" Essay

I agree with the quote that problems are opportunities in disguise. Sometimes problems are opportunities, too.

I have a lot of problems like anyone else does. Sometimes there very difficult and I don't no how to handle them. When I have a really big problem, I sometimes ask my parents or freinds for advise. Sometimes they help, sometimes they don't, then I have to figure out how to handle it myself.

One time I had a big problem. Where someone stole my wallet and I had to get to a job interview. But I had no money and no ID. This happen in school. So I went to the principles office and reported it. He called the man I was supposed to interview with. Who rescheduled the intervew for me. So I still had the opportunity to interview and I'm proud to say I got the job. In fact I'm still working there!

Problems can be opportunities if you just look at them that way. Instead of the other way around.

SET 46 (Page 149)

480.
Sample "6" Essay

Courage and cowardice seem like absolutes. We are often quick to label other people, or ourselves, as either "brave" or "timid," "courageous" or "cowardly." However, one bright afternoon on a river deep in the wilds of the Ozark mountains, I learned that these qualities are as changeable as mercury.

During a cross-country drive, my friend Nina and I decided to stop at a campsite in Missouri and spend the afternoon on a boat trip down Big Piney River, 14 miles through the wilderness. We rented a canoe and paddled happily off. Things were fine for the first seven or eight miles. We gazed at the overhanging bluffs, commented on the dogwoods in bloom, and marveled at the clarity of the water. Then, in approaching Devil's Elbow, a bend in the river, the current suddenly swept us in toward the bank, under the low-hanging branches of a weeping willow. The canoe tipped over, and I was pulled under. My foot caught for just a few seconds on the willow's submerged roots, and just as I surfaced, I saw the canoe sweeping out, upright again, but empty. Nina was frantically swimming after it.

Standing by cravenly, I knew I should help, but I was petrified. I let my friend brave the treacherous rapids and haul the canoe back onto the gravel bar by herself. But then came the scream, and Nina dashed back into the water. In the bottom of the canoe, a black and brown, checkerboard-patterned copperhead snake lay coiled. I don't know exactly why, but the inborn terror of snakes is something that has passed me by completely. I actually find them rather charming in a scaly sort of way, but Nina was still screaming. In a calm way that must have seemed smug, I said, "We're in its home, it's not in ours." And gently, I prodded it with the oar until it reared up, slithered over the side of the canoe, and raced away.

Later that night, in our cozy, safe motel room, we agreed that we each had cold chills thinking about what might have happened. Still, I learned something important from the ordeal. I know that, had we encountered only the rapids, I might have come away ashamed, labeling myself a coward, and had we encountered only the snake, Nina might have done the same. I also know that neither of us will ever again be quite so apt to brand another person as lacking courage. Because we will always know that, just around the corner, may be the snake or the bend in the river or the figure in the shadows or something else as yet unanticipated, that will cause our own blood to freeze.

Sample "4" Essay

Courage can be shown in many ways and by many kinds of people. One does not have to be rich, or educated, or even an adult to show true courage.

For example, a very heartbreaking thing happened in our family. It turned out all right but at the time it almost made us lose our faith. However, it also taught us a lesson regarding courage. In spite of his father's and my repeated warnings, my son Matt went ice-fishing with some friends and fell through the ice into the frigid water beneath. He is prone to do things that are dangerous no matter how many times he's told. Fortunately there were grown-ups near and they were able to throw him a life line and pull him to safety. However, when they got him onto shore they discovered he was unconscious. There were vital signs but they were weak, the paramedics pronounced him in grave danger.

He is his little sisters (Nans) hero. He is 16 and she is 13, just at the age where she admires everything he does. When they took him to the hospital she insisted on going that night to see him, and she insisted on staying with me there. My husband thought we should insist she go home, but it was Christmas vacation for her so there was no real reason. So we talked it over and she stayed. She stayed every night for the whole week just to be by Matt's side. And when he woke up she was there. Her smiling face the was first thing he saw.

In spite of the fact she was just a child and it was frightning for her to be there beside her brother she loves so much, and had to wonder, every day if he would die, she stayed. So courage has many faces.

Sample "3" Essay

Courage is not something we are born with. It is something that we have to learn.

For example when your children are growing up you should teach them courage. Teach them to face lifes challanges and not to show there fear. For instance my father. Some people would say he was harsh, but back then I didnt think of it that way. One time he took me camping and I had a tent of my own. I wanted to crawl in with him but he said there was nothing to be afriad of. And I went to sleep sooner than I would have expect. He taught me not to be afriad.

There are many reasons for courage. In a war a solder has to be couragous and a mother has to be no less couragous if she is rasing a child alone and has to make a living. So, in me it is totally alright to be afriad as long as you face your fear. I have been greatful to him ever since that night.

Sometimes parents know what is best for there kids even if at the time it seems like a harsh thing. I learned not to show my fear that night, which is an important point to courage. In everyday life it is important to learn how to be strong. If we dont learn from our parents, like I did from my father, then we have to learn it after we grow up. But it is better to learn it, as a child. I have never been as afriad as I was that night, and I learned a valuble lesson from it.

Sample "1" Essay

Courage is important in a battle and also ordinary life. In a war if your buddy depends on you and you let him down he might die. Courage is also important in daly life. If you have sicknes in the famly or if you enconter a mugger on the street you will need all the courage you can get. There are many dangers in life that only courage will see you through.

Once, my apartment was burglerised and they stole a TV and microwave. I didnt have very much. They took some money to. I felt afraid when I walked in and saw things moved or gone. But I call the police and waited for them inside my apartment which was brave and also some might say stupid! But the police came and took my statement and also later caught the guy. Another time my girlfreind and I were in my apartment and we looked out the window and there was somebody suspisious out in front. It turned out to be a false alarm but she was scard and she said because I was calm it made her feel better. So courage was important to me, in my relatinship with my girlfeind.

So courage is importand not only in war but also in life.

481.

Sample "6" Essay

Writing can be taught, at least the kind of basic composition needed to be successful in school. The most important factor in teaching a basic composition class is a simple one for students who have been less than successful writers in the past. The student should be asked to write about something interesting in a context with a purpose beyond "English class." In other words, the student should *want* to learn to write. For students who have fallen behind for one reason or another, it's difficult to see a writing class as anything but an exercise in plummeting self-esteem. Many students believe that writing well is a mystery only those "with talent" can understand, and that "English class" is just something to endure. The first thing to teach students is that writing has a purpose that pertains to their lives. The teacher must appeal to emotion as well as to intellect.

I believe that the best approach is to ask students to keep a journal in two parts. In one part, grammar and style shouldn't matter, the way they have to matter in the formal assignments that come later in the course. In this part of the journal, the students should be asked to keep track of things they encounter during the day that interest them or cause them to be happy, sad, angry, or afraid. In the second part of the journal they should keep track of subjects that make them sit up and take notice. These can include things that happen in class or ideas that come to them when reading an assignment for class. These journal notes should whet the intellect and excite curiosity.

For teaching grammar, the teacher can present exercises in the context of a one-page essay or story because it gives writing a context. Too often in the early grades, students complete dry drill and skill exercises that take the fun out of writing. Diagramming sentences, identifying nouns and verbs, or labeling adjectives seems far removed from the skill of writing. Appeal to emotion, intellect, and curiosity will really succeed in engaging the whole student and awakening the urge to write.

Sample "4" Essay

I believe writing can be taught if we work hard enough at it as teachers. The important thing is to teach students that it can be enjoyable. Years of fearing writing lie behind a lot of students, and it's one of the biggest stumbling blocks. But it can be gotten over.

Having them break up into small groups is one way to teach writing to reluctant or ill-prepared students. Have the students discuss a topic they are all interested in—say a recent TV show or an event coming up at school, then plan a paper and come back and discuss the idea with the whole class. Your next step can be to have them actually write the paper, then get into their small groups again and criticize what theyve done.

Another way for students who don't like the small groups is one on one conferences. But dont just talk about grammar or sentence structure or paragraphing, talk about the content of his paper. I did a summer internship teaching in an innter city school, and I rememmber one young man. He hated small groups so we talked privately. He had written a paper on going to a city-sponsored camping trip and seeing white-tailed deer, which was his first time. He was excited about it, and I suggested he write a paper about his experience. He did and, except for some trouble with grammar, it was an A paper, full of active verbs and telling detail!

Finally, try to get your students to read. If you have to, drag them to the community library yourself. Not only will it help their writing, it will help them in life. Only by getting them interested in the written word and by helping them to see that it matters in their everyday lives can you really reach them and set them on the path of good writing.

Yes. Writing can be taught if you are willing to take the time and do the hard work and maybe give a few extra hours. No student is hopeless. And writing is so important in today's world that its worth the extra effort.

Sample "3" Essay

I dont think writing can be taught neccesarily, although if the students are half-way motivated anything's possible. The first thing is get them interested in the subject and give them alot of writing to do in class. They may not do it if it is all outside class as many poorly prepared students hate homework. I know I did as a kid!

Writing does not come natural for most people especially in the poorer school districs. Unless they are lucky enough to have parents who read to them. That is another aspect of teaching how to write. Assign alot of reading. If you don't read you can't write, and that is lacking in alot of students backgrounds. If your students wont' read books tell them to read comic books if nothing else. Anything to get them to read.

The second thing is to have the student come in for a conference once a week. That is one way to see what is going on with them in school and at home. A lot of kids in the poorer schools have conflict at home and that is why they fail. So give them alot of praise because thats what they need.

Finaly don't give up. It can be done. Many people born into poverty go on to do great things. You can help and you never know who you will inspire and who will remember you as the best teacher they ever had.

Sample "1" Essay

You will be able to tell I am one of the peopel that never learned to write well. I wish I had but my personal experience as a struggeling writer will inspire my students, thats the most I can hope for. Writing can be taught, but you have to be ready to inspire the student. Give them assignments on subjets they like and keep after them to read. Take them to the public libary if they havnt been and introduce them to books.

If you cant write people will call you dumb or stupid which hurts you're self-estem. I know from experience.

The next thing is have them come in and talk to you. You never know what is going on in there lifes that is keeping them from studying and doing there best. Maybe they have a mom that works all the time or a dad who has left the home. Be sure to teach the whole person. Also have them write about what is going on in there lives, not a dry subject like the drinking age. Have the student write about there personal experience and it will come out better. Writing can be taught if the student is motivated. So hang in there.

Grade Yourself

These sample essays show you how the scoring guide works. There are no sample essays for the rest of the topics in Section 6. Simply use the scoring rubric on pages 198–199 to evaluate your essays. Remember, it's better to have someone else read your essay than to try to evaluate it yourself.

Additional Online Practice

Whether you need help building basic skills or preparing for an exam, visit the LearningExpress Practice Center! On this site, you can access additional practice materials. Using the code below, you'll be able to log in and answer even more grammar and writing practice questions. This online practice will also provide you with:

- **Immediate scoring**
- **Detailed answer explanations**
- **Personalized recommendations for further practice and study**

Log in to the LearningExpress Practice Center by using this URL: **www.learnatest.com/practice**

This is your Access Code: **7489**

Follow the steps online to redeem your access code. After you've used your access code to register with the site, you will be prompted to create a username and password. For easy reference, record them here:

Username: _____ **Password:** _____

With your username and password, you can log in and access the additional practice questions. If you have any questions or problems, please contact LearningExpress customer service at 1-800-295-9556 ext. 2, or e-mail us at **customerservice@learningexpressllc.com**.